SWIMMING
UPSTREAM

SWIMMING UPSTREAM

My Struggle and Triumph Over Cancer and the Medical Establishment:
New Hope in Cancer Treatment

Sajjad Iqbal, M.D.

ISBN: 1539983544
ISBN 13: 9781539983545
Library of Congress Control Number: 2016919580
CreateSpace Independent Publishing Platform
North Charleston, South Carolina

In loving memory of my parents,
Kulsoom Akhtar and Pir Muhammad Iqbal.
I owe everything to their love, nurturing, and guidance.

ACKNOWLEDGMENTS

There are so many people who have helped me throughout my journey, too many to be named here. You know who you are, and you have my unwavering respect and appreciation for being a part of the most important time of my life.

The love of my life—my soul mate for the last forty-two wonderful years—Fauzia, has also endured all the trials and tribulations while standing firmly beside me. Her selfless love and support has been my lifeblood through extremely difficult and anguished times during this long struggle against the deadliest of enemies. Fauzia has also been the source of the greatest joys and heavenly blissful times in my life. I remain eternally grateful to her and humbled by her grace during all of this.

My exceptional family continues to inspire me. That includes my amazing children, Sheeraz, Noreen, and Daniyal. Each of them makes me so proud every single day. My two lovely little grandkids, Deen and Hana, have provided a perfect antidote to any stress, anxiety, or sadness. There is an unbreakable bond between siblings, and mine have been my strength, especially my elder brother Javed, who is my own personal guardian angel.

Thank you to my friend and advisor Tom McCarthy. Without his invaluable help and guidance during the entire process, this book would never have materialized. He is responsible for shaping my voice and maintaining the integrity of my story.

Thank you also to my good friend Phaedra Cress, who was always there for me whenever I needed her advice or help and who did a remarkable job of both developmental editing and copyediting on the manuscript.

I extend my gratitude to Komal Ali and Noreen Iqbal, for reading the manuscript chapter by chapter as it was being written and for giving such valuable feedback.

Lastly, I would like to thank the two amazing physicians who literally saved my life: Dr. Barry Schaitkin, my surgeon at UPMC-Shadyside Medical Center, and Dr. Indu Sharma, my oncologist for the last ten years. As you can see from reading this book, I am alive today because of these two kind, competent, and compassionate physicians. I am eternally grateful to them.

And to all the readers who will travel beside me while reading about my journey and who may be able to help others or themselves during a similar experience with cancer, thank you for listening and reading. Never give up hope. Follow your instincts and believe in yourself, even when you are a single reed swaying in a field of strangers.

CONTENTS

FOREWORD

Finding a Zebra Among Horses
Barry M Schaitkin, MD

I am a better doctor for having met Sajjad Iqbal and I appreciate that he took the time to so articulately retell the story of his illness.

I remember quite clearly my first visit with Dr. Sajjad Iqbal. We had spoken by phone and arranged for him to visit me. I was immediately impressed with his soft but articulate presentation of his own case, his documentation of every aspect, and the way he had continued to move the ball forward by himself. He always demanded honest but well-reasoned thinking about the implications of each aspect of his illness to allow a furthering of the assault against his cancer. He is clearly only alive today because he took on this challenge. However, to be fair, he presented with an uncommon problem and was repeatedly given the common diagnosis. There is a saying in medical school that if one is out in a field and hears hoof beats from behind, it is best to think of a horse not a zebra; but of course, there are always zebras. Sajjad's case was a zebra. More importantly, if one listened very closely to the story it never really sounded like hoof beats. He had a kind of facial paralysis that was different in presentation from the common viral Bell's palsy. I had the amazing good fortune to study the presentation of facial paralysis from Dr. Mark May, now retired, who was—and remains—the foremost authority on the subject in the world. It made me a better listener.

Dr. Iqbal has beautifully shared for us all his early beginnings, his family, and his cancer story. It is a most inspiring tale of the importance of parenting, family, professionalism, training, work ethic, struggle, persistence, and wisdom—with multiple peaks and valleys along the way and more yet to come. I am honored to have met his family and shared in his story. I am happy to have contributed to it, and am humbled by the most generous treatment I have been given by the author in his memoir.

Unfortunately, Sajjad is not the only patient with a parotid cancer to have presented to me in this manner. This is why this book is so vitally important to doctors—because it reminds us all that no matter what clinical condition we treat, we will be wrong! It is impossible to see patients every day and not miss something or make wrong decisions. Only the vain would dare admit otherwise. Even careful doctors can be led astray by a rush to judgment, a tactile misstep, or from an incorrectly read X-ray or biopsy specimen pathology report. When the patient's history does not make sense and is outside the normal "horse" diagnosis, one should honestly say, "I don't know what is wrong." At that point it behooves us all to continue to follow closely, to order additional studies, or to refer to someone else to get a fresh set of eyes to look at the problem. We should always be thinking: it could be a zebra.

This book is also a beautiful gift from the author to all the patients lucky enough to read it. It is a testimony to the powers of luck, hard work, positive attitude, and medical innovation. Like my now deceased father who was kept alive by cardiac innovations that kept evolving with his needs for them, Sajjad's happy story is also dependent on the time period during which he developed his illness and the remarkable progress in cancer therapies over the past decade. There is inspiration and knowledge that can be gleaned from this story by patients and family members alike, and I know that Sajjad's greatest joy will be in knowing, or probably in just believing, that his struggle will ease the path of those yet to come. There is always hope and his story is living proof.

PROLOGUE

November 2012

I was sitting in my car in an emptying parking lot outside my radiologist's office as the business day wound to an end in the unadorned northern New Jersey city of Hackensack, a place most people drive past on the way to somewhere else without taking notice. The town is primarily known for the excellent hospital, Hackensack University Medical Center, and the county courthouse. Neither place is somewhere you want to find yourself.

The contrasts were stark. Perhaps they would have even been comical if they had not come after the unambiguous verdict that announced itself so clearly in my latest bone scan. My ten-year battle with cancer was not yet over, as I had thought and hoped it would be.

The war would continue, it seemed. The remission I had hoped was a permanent victory had merely been a temporary truce. For a moment, I allowed myself to wander aimlessly, taking in the gravity of this news and allowing myself this brief moment to come to terms with what I had just learned, to have this time alone to process it and be calm.

Hackensack, a gritty and energetic community, has its attractions, I suppose. But it has never been called a place of pastoral beauty and serenity. Yet as I sat in my car, I was strangely at peace and in awe of the beauty around me.

When I had seen the scans, I had known immediately what they meant. I got into my car, took a deep breath, and looked around. Nearby buildings were backlit by a calming orange glow as the sun set that November evening in 2012. The air was crisp, clean, and refreshing. The chatter from the McDonald's next door was actually amusing, and the cacophony of the traffic on Essex Street a block away was wonderful. I could hear birds chirping in trees that were shedding leaves in the fading light.

It was all nothing short of beautiful. As I sat there, I was overcome with a sense of tranquility. Hackensack, the traffic, the noise, the birds, the trees, and the setting sun— God's earth was beautiful. Hackensack was beautiful. I chuckled. Of all places to find beauty!

I would miss this, I thought. My life was coming to an end. For a moment, my heart sank a bit—but only briefly.

As the newly recognized beauty of Hackensack washed over me, I was surprised that even though I knew the cancer was back and the prognosis was grim, the only thing I felt was a rather peculiar sadness. I realized I might be coming to the end of my life, but I was also aware that I felt no panic, no anxiety, and no grief. It was a calm kind of sadness. I wasn't quite ready to surrender. "I shall fight," I thought, but I was also completely at peace with whatever might happen in the future. I felt two wildly contrasting emotions, a strong will to fight for my life yet a willingness to surrender to my fate.

Then came what you would expect. "Now what am I going to do?"

As a physician, I knew what it all meant. After all, I had been fighting cancer at this point for years. In fact, at the beginning, I had to take extraordinary measures just to get the specialists to listen, to recognize the symptoms for what they were, and to treat them properly. That had been a struggle, but I had overcome their blinding arrogance and resistance and I had reached a point only five months before where I had been declared cancer-free after a long fight.

In January 2012, I'd begun to experience paralysis of the left vocal cord, perhaps a by-product of the years of treatment I had undergone for cancer of my parotid gland—the salivary gland. This vocal cord paralysis made it increasingly difficult for me to speak. I'd had a minor procedure, an injection into the vocal cord, in April, but the condition worsened to the point that in July doctors had recommended a more extensive surgery. That option came with a caveat: we will do it only if you are cancer-free. The implication, of course, was that there was no point in having the surgery if I was dying of cancer.

That July, I had a CT scan that showed no signs of cancer in my chest, abdomen, pelvis, or the surrounding bones. I was cancer-free and good to go.

I had the surgery at New York University Medical Center on October 19 and was home by October 23. The

pain started almost immediately, and I had wishfully at-
tributed it to the uncomfortable hospital bed. But it continued, and as a physician, I knew that if it continued,
there might be something wrong, though I didn't want to
jump the gun.

I called a chiropractor friend and asked him to try to
alleviate the pain, but being a realist, I told him he had two
weeks. "If you can't fix it in two weeks," I said, "I'm afraid I
might be in trouble." I have always had a good sense of my
body, always felt in tune with what was going on, and when
the pain persisted, I knew it was time for a bone scan, which
is what led me to the parking lot in Hackensack.

The night before the bone scan, on November 15, 2012,
I was sitting in my study at home in front of the computer,
sharpening my knowledge of bone scans and learning how
they could differentiate between cancer and, say, arthritis,
which certainly would have been a more benign and acceptable outcome.

My wife of thirty-eight years, Fauzia, who had suffered
as only the loved ones of cancer patients can—wanting
to help in every way but finding herself utterly helpless—
walked in and saw what I was looking at. She immediately
began crying.

"Do you think you have cancer again?" she asked.

"No, I'm just trying to refresh my knowledge," I said
rather pointlessly since she already knew. I was trying to
spare her another day of pain and suffering, but after so
many years together, she could read me like a book.

After the scan the next day, I had walked over to the radiologist and we looked together as he put it up on the screen.

Right away, I could see what he was seeing: several areas of cancer nodules in my spine, ribs, and pelvic area, five of them. He pointed them out. "Here and here and here and here."

I nodded my head.

He put his arm around my shoulders as we sat in front of the screen.

"I am so sorry, Dr. Iqbal. I wish I could tell you something better."

"Thank you," I said. "I'm not sorry. I'm not even terribly upset. I expected this. It's just another battle in this ongoing war. I just have to fight again."

After I went to my car in the parking lot, startled at the newfound beauty of a fall evening in Hackensack, I immediately began planning my next move. Everyone in my family would be waiting for the news.

I didn't want to call Fauzia at work, knowing how upset she would be. She would be home in an hour, and I would tell her then, I thought.

I called my son Sheeraz, a pediatrician. I knew he'd be wrapping up his office hours by then.

He picked up the phone, and his first words were, "What does it show?"

I will never forget the first penetrating silence after I told him, followed by his anguished voice. I could actually hear him slump down hard in a chair.

"Oh no. Oh God, no."

"Sheeraz," I said, "don't be upset. This is nothing new. We have fought this before, and this is just another battle in the ongoing war; we'll figure something out. I will be home soon."

Next, I called my oncologist, Dr. Indu Sharma, who was just about to leave her office. I told her the news.

"This is bad news," she said. "There is no standard treatment, as you already know, but we'll try to figure something out. I'll do a literature search over the weekend and get back to you."

Next I called my office manager of twenty-five years, Pat, who was also a dear friend and always seemed to worry about me. I dialed her cell phone, and when she picked up, she was crying.

"I know! I know!" she said in between her sobs. "I was there when Sheeraz got the call. I just picked up my pocketbook and ran out crying."

"There is nothing to cry about. I will be fine," I said.

Sitting there, I decided not to call my other two children. Noreen worked in New York City, and I'd tell her the news when she got back to her apartment. My youngest son, Daniyal, was in Boston studying for law school finals, and I felt no need to distract him. "I can tell him when he's home over Thanksgiving break," I reasoned.

So I drove home, feeling numb.

When I got home, there was a pall over everything. Fauzia wanted to know, and I sat her down and told her. The news met with predicable results.

"Don't worry; we'll figure a way," I said.

When I called Noreen, she immediately started to cry.

"There is nothing to cry about, my love," I told her.

"But, Dad, we don't want to lose you," she said through sobs.

"I don't want to lose myself," I replied.

Then it struck me how dumb that phrase was, and I added, "Noreen, what I meant is I don't want to die either. We will fight it and conquer it again."

But no matter what I said, there was a deep, deep gloom over the household.

Sheeraz gave Fauzia something to help her sleep, but that night, no one slept in the Iqbal household.

Except me. I slept like a baby.

CHAPTER 1

THE FOUNDATION—GIFTS FROM MY ANCESTORS

I have a slightly faded black-and-white photograph of my father. He is fashionably turned out in a stylishly cut three-piece suit. In the photo, taken around 1937, the contrasts of his dark suit are set off cleanly by a pressed white shirt. Everything is in its place, impeccable. My father, standing erect but relaxed and confident, is wearing a bow tie and smiling serenely. He is standing on a railway platform from the looks of it, possibly Shahdara Junction, one of the many depots where he served as stationmaster in what was still India at that time. He was in his late twenties then, a young man on the rise.

The photo shows his handsomeness and perhaps, if you knew him, his charm.

What it doesn't show is his resoluteness and his unimpeachable sense of right and wrong, his solidness. It hints but does not show that standing on that railroad platform is a man of principle who would, through his own determined efforts and sense of obligation, support his large family of siblings, reject the religious hatred and violence that would soon consume his contemporaries, and teach his children, me included, that there is no ambiguity when it comes to weighing questions of morality. He would teach all his children, by example more than formal lectures, that there is right and there is wrong. There are no gray areas.

When I look at that photo now, what I see is not my father as a young man but rather a man who gave to me the wonderful gifts that have carried me through some difficult times of my own when I was a much older man than he was in that photo. My struggle with cancer, in fact my initial struggle to even get the proper diagnosis of what was troubling me, was undertaken with a solid and unshakable conviction that if things—even potentially lethal crises— are handled calmly and rationally, grace will prevail.

The unblemished fortitude and determination that carried me during my cancer struggle was a gift from my father, Muhammad Iqbal, and my mother, Kulsoom. My parents were a perfect complement for each other, and they provided me with the love, security, and self-assurance that served me well both in good times and bad.

Undoubtedly, and without hyperbole, I believe I had the best parents in the world, the best way of growing up anyone could ask for. I am lucky in that respect. And that gift extended itself later to my own family, which was and is a gift better than I deserved. As I look back from this brighter end of my long medical struggle, my three wonderful children, my wife, my siblings—even my extended circle of friends—provided me with an energy during my cancer fight that was stronger than any drug or any treatment regimen. They provided an inner strength when mine was ebbing.

Friends who see that photograph of my father on the railway platform these days are often taken aback by the understated glamour of the man on the railway platform. "Who is that man?" they will inevitably ask.

He was bright and dashing and unabashedly progressive at a time in Punjab when tradition dictated nearly every social and religious behavior, a time in which Muslims and Hindus and Sikhs lived tenuously, almost precariously, together with thinly hidden enmity. It was a time when the soon-to-crumble British Raj still held sway over the subcontinent. The sun, the British once proudly said, never sets on the empire. But in India after World War II, when I was born in Sialkot, Punjab, in the new country of Pakistan, the sun was setting quickly, and the darkness in those early days would have consumed my family had it not been for the brightness of my parents, uncles, and extended family.

My father was, by all accounts, a terrific son. The oldest of his siblings, he quit his college studies when he realized it was his duty to care for four brothers and five sisters. One of his brothers, my uncle Hamid, was considered a brilliant scholar and wanted to attend college. My father took as his responsibility the work of making sure Hamid completed his college studies. As his sisters became old enough to marry, he saw it as his job to bear the bulk of the financial burden for their weddings. He was a selfless man, and when he took a job with the railways, he rose quickly.

All this occurred before I was born in 1947. Before the subcontinent was torn apart by a violence so wretched that the hatred is still thick today, seventy years later. My father's family was fortunate. They were Muslims in a Muslim area that would become Pakistan and were not uprooted. Not every Muslim was this lucky.

That year, 1947, was officially known as "the Partition of India," an innocuous enough sounding term applied by politicians to a time of great and tragic unrest in which India was split into the Muslim Pakistan and predominately Hindu India, though Sikhs sought refuge in the new India as well.

The years between the end of World War II and the partition were fraught with tension as various parties on both side of the issue struggled to allocate assets and territory between centuries-old antagonists. And as with most political struggles, it was the poorer people who suffered the greatest loss and endured the most heinous violence.

Millions of other Muslims were trapped on the "wrong" side of the border, in India. As they tried to make their way to the promised land of Pakistan, by trains, buses, or bullock carts but mostly on foot, they were routinely attacked by crazed and armed Sikh or Hindu mobs. "Ghost trains" from India arrived in Sialkot or Lahore on a daily basis—trains full of dead and mutilated bodies, hundreds upon hundreds of men, women, and children, even infants, slaughtered by the crazed mobs who often allowed only the driver to live so he could deliver this grotesque message to the other side.

Similarly, millions of Hindus and Sikhs woke up one day and suddenly found themselves in a new and hostile land. Neighbors and friends with whom they had coexisted for generations were now after their blood. Their houses were burned down, possessions looted, men murdered, and women raped or killed. Attempting to escape to India, they often suffered a fate very similar to that of their Muslim counterparts trying to migrate to Pakistan. A complete and total madness prevailed.

Punjab was once a little slice of heaven. The devil himself could not have imagined a place more hellish than the Punjab of 1947.

While Muslims and Hindus and Sikhs were killing each other with predictable regularity, my father and his family made it a daily practice, at their own peril, to save as many people as possible from the senseless crazed mobs who attacked those unfortunate enough to be caught in their paths.

My father's family had come to the area a few generations before. Sialkot, a city of greenery in the northeast Punjab, played an important role in the creation of Pakistan, hosting several pivotal meetings. It is now a major industrial center of Pakistan, but it wasn't at that time. It sits on the border of Kashmir, which even today is the source of great friction and occasional skirmishes between Indian and Pakistani forces. Some things never change, I suppose.

But the point was, as my mother told me later, my family was established and respected enough in the area to be able to assert itself, to take the great risk of bucking the accepted hatred and reaching out to help the Hindus and Sikhs who might otherwise have been killed, as so many were in those days.

That is the legacy handed down to me, I feel—family, integrity, deep love of all things right, and calmness under pressure. It seems to me that those relatives were diligent and unambiguous in doing what they had to do when it would have been much easier and politically expedient to fade into the background and let the violence take its course.

"It is not in our blood to be dishonest," my father once told me.

By the time I was born in Sialkot, the explosive violence of the partition had already burst out and affected everyone. It was an unspeakably ugly time, when thousands of Hindus and Sikhs and Muslims were displaced as territories were shuffled and the new countries were established. In textbooks, the idea of partition was a master stroke, neat and efficient. The reality, of course, was far different and more visceral. And as political architects often are, the politicians who designed the partition were unprepared for the actual results. The newly formed governments in Pakistan and India were completely unequipped to deal with the forced migrations and—there is no better description for it—the staggering levels of slaughter and violence that occurred on both sides of the new borders. Riots in the Punjab before the partition killed between 200,000 and 500,000 people in what was termed "retributive genocide." People were forced to move because of religion; by some estimates, some fourteen million Hindus, Sikhs, and Muslims were uprooted during the partition—considered the largest mass migration in human history. And it was not a gentle and peaceful uprooting.

Hindu and Sikh families who had lived in the area around Sialkot for generations were forced to move. And they moved at great risk to their lives, their fortunes, and their emotional health.

"There was madness on both sides," my mother would later recall. "But we tried to take care of the Hindus."

Because we were Muslims in a Muslim area, we were safe. It was the Hindus and Sikhs who were being slaughtered in our area. The hordes of Muslims coming in from India with horrific stories of the rape, murder, and looting they had experienced exacerbated violence toward Hindus and Sikhs in many parts of Pakistan, including Sialkot.

My uncle Hamid, the brother my father put through college, was a physically dominant presence—a fierce man with unshakable ideals. He would often be seen with my cousin Ishaq, himself no shrinking violet.

The two of them were, my mother said, expert horsemen and an intimidating pair. They would head out night after night, patrolling Hindu communities and, if necessary, repelling marauding mobs looking for Hindu blood. If that meant injecting themselves at some peril in the fray, so be it. Hamid and Ishaq themselves would return, often at dawn, exhausted and covered in blood from the night's activities.

I had heard these stories for years, and for the most part, I had always been skeptical. Too pat, too heroic, unlikely, I thought. The stories of their nightly fights seemed to me too contrived to be true. I mentioned that recently to my oldest brother, Sarfraz, and he assured me not only that it was true but also that he was an eyewitness to it.

Sarfraz was only a teenager then, yet he desperately wanted to join Hamid and Ishaq on their heroic missions. They always refused his requests, saying Sarfraz was too young to be exposed to such dangers, until one evening when they finally relented. That night, Sarfraz, Hamid, and Ishaq saved a Hindu woman whose husband had just been killed by a mob that was planning to subject her to the same brutality. But they were able to send the mob away and save her life, at no small risk to their own. After the mob dispersed, the grateful and tearful woman went into her house and brought out an ornate, solid-gold necklace, likely a family heirloom.

"My gratitude to the special mother who has raised such sons," she said as she handed the necklace to Sarfraz.

When my brother brought the necklace to my mother, she angrily admonished him for snatching the necklace from some desperate woman.

After my brother explained that the precious necklace was actually a gift for her from a grateful woman whose life they had saved, my mother still refused to accept it.

"You go back right now," she said, "and tell the woman that she is in no position to give such gifts. This necklace would help her start a new life in India," she added.

That's how my parents were, and I have so much admiration for them because of it.

Later, when I was five or six, I became aware and attracted to a huge book my father kept on top of a large walnut bureau in our house, out of reach from my curious hands. I was attracted to the book whenever my father pulled it from the top of the bureau and carefully, reverently, dusted it. I could see its beautiful blue, red, and yellow drawings and ornate writing. It was to a young boy a huge treasure, thick and maybe two feet square.

"What is that book?" I wondered.

I thought at first it might be a Quran, but it wasn't, my father told me.

It was a Granth Sahib, a collection of teachings and writings by ten gurus, saints of the Sikh religion. These scriptures were written in Punjabi and are greatly respected by all Sikhs as the living word of God.

Why did we have it? And why was my father, a Muslim, taking such gentle care of it?

It seems that shortly after the Sikhs and Hindus had left Sialkot, he had once stopped to buy some roasted peanuts from a street-side shop and saw that the nuts were wrapped indifferently by the shopkeeper in the ornate pages of what my father immediately recognized as the Granth Sahib. To the shopkeeper, those holy pages were nothing more than a convenient way to sell and wrap his goods—trash, really.

He bought the book from the surprised shopkeeper and brought it home.

"What are you going to do with it?" the shopkeeper asked.

"This is precious to someone, and I will take care of it until the rightful owners come back."

After years of watching my father mindfully and gently dust that holy book, I asked him one day why he cared for the Granth Sahib when it was not his holy book. "My son," my father said, "if we want others to respect our religion, we must respect theirs first."

When I was about ten, my father met a Sikh traveling from India at his railway station. He told him about the book and brought him to our house to show him. When he pulled the book down from the top of the bureau and showed the man, the surprised and grateful visitor bent slowly over it, in tears, and kissed it.

My father gave it to him. "Now, I have discharged my obligation," my father said.

Though I didn't know it at the time, my father was providing me with the grounding that would serve me so well later as I made my way through school and medical school and after I moved to America.

My father passed away suddenly and unexpectedly in January 1975. A few days after his passing, a blind man approached our house one morning and started tapping on my father's bedroom window, asking for his "monthly stipend." My brother Mansoor went out to investigate. Turns out that for years my father had financially supported this poor blind man and his family. Mansoor gave him the money and told him to keep coming. His monthly stipend would always be waiting for him.

Such was the generosity of my father.

When it comes to generosity, hardly anyone could match my mother. She was kind, loving, and compassionate toward anyone and everyone she met but particularly so toward the poor, the needy, the downtrodden, and the sick. No one who came to her door, whether a relative in need or a stranger seeking alms, left without my mother thrusting some money into his or her hands. She would literally give someone the shirt off her back—and she did just that. My brother Javed gave her a very nice and warm woolen sweater, which she loved. Then one day, she saw an old lady who had served our family for a while, shivering in an unexpectedly bitter cold spell in Karachi. She took her favorite sweater off and handed it to the poor woman despite the protests of her daughter-in-law Shahida. "She needs it more," said my mother.

Those were subtle, living gifts presented to me simply by the way my parents lived, the way they treated and cared for people, and the way they carried themselves—confident but never arrogant, self-assured, but always respectful of the opinions of others. These were the best kinds of gifts taught through example and love as the right way to live.

They would serve me well later, when I was closer to dying than I cared to admit.

CHAPTER 2
AN UNINVITED GUEST

October 2000

The first jolt, a rude and unwelcome intrusion, came unexpectedly, as most jolts usually do.

A sharp, piercing pain below my left ear woke me from my usual pleasant and undisturbed sleep very early on the morning of October 26, 2000, a Saturday that I hoped would provide me the rare chance to sleep in, if only for a bit.

If I thought anything at that instant, it was a fleeting sense that I might need to get up and take something to get back to sleep. Toothache? Ear infection?

Before that rude autumn morning awakening, life could not have been better for me. At fifty-four, my pediatrics practice in Ridgewood, New Jersey—a leafy and pleasant suburb a stone's throw from New York City—was flourishing. I had been drawn to Ridgewood in 1976, and with my growing family had settled there permanently with an office in our home in 1988. I loved pediatrics and drew great energy from helping children and easing the worries of concerned parents. And I loved the home office, a situation I often described as an ideal commute in an area full of working people often driving through very congested communities or taking crowded trains into New York City.

I was as busy as I wanted to be. My children were advancing through school, and my determined and incredibly strong wife had just received her master's degree the previous May.

Fauzia had dropped out of college when we married in 1974. Between giving birth to our children and holding full-time jobs while being a wife and mother, she had continued to take college courses, the culmination of which was a master's degree. She graduated from nearby Ramapo College, a small but highly regarded institution. I was an extremely proud husband.

As the children were growing up, our daughter Noreen had at one point developed a strong childhood affinity for the actress Helen Slater, who played Supergirl in a popular film of 1984. I can still recall saying to her, "Supergirl? You don't need to go to the movies to see her. You have Superwoman right here. Your mother."

On the morning that prompted my first tentative step in the long journey to learn the precise cause of my growing health problems, all my children were doing well. My son Sheeraz was studying medicine at St. George's University School of Medicine and was completing a clinical rotation at Jamaica Hospital in nearby Queens, New York. Noreen, by that time no longer in awe of Supergirl, was in her second year at NYU, and our youngest son, Daniyal, was eleven and in middle school in Ridgewood.

Fauzia and I had a pleasantly active social life and a terrific group of supportive and entertaining friends. Though I had never been driven by or even remotely obsessed with money, my investments were moving comfortably in the right direction, upward and steady.

Life was wonderful.

My health had never been an issue. In fact, I used to joke with friends that I was "disgustingly healthy." Up until that fall morning in 2000, I had never even had an accident or needed stitches.

As sagas often begin, there was not a dark cloud in sight. My life was nothing short of perfect, I thought. Little did I know how radically it was about to change.

I am not nor have I ever been an alarmist, a trait that emerged both from my affection for logic—my faith that problems can be solved calmly by analysis—and from my simple joy at life in general.

It might even be something I inherited from my father, who once saved a small town, literally, when I was about ten years old.

Alarmed by a series of cries from bystanders as he looked off his station platform one afternoon during his rounds, he was shocked to see that a nearby house was engulfed in flames. He noticed, too, how close the house was to the large oil-storage depot at which tanker cars from the railroad frequently stopped. Between the two, like stepping-stones, was a string of easily ignited and flammable barrels of fuel, waiting to be loaded on the next train. It was a potentially lethal combination.

If one of those barrels had been caught up in the flames, it would have sparked a chain reaction causing oblivion for the house and the storage tank, maybe even the train station and the neighborhood.

My father stepped from the platform, and while alarmed bystanders cried out for him to stop, he stepped perilously close to the raging fire and began to methodically and calmly roll the barrels away from the path of the flames.

Terrified and frozen in place, I heard the crowd screaming, "No! Sir, no! Come back! It is suicidal."

But he continued to remove the barrels from the flame's path, helping a community to avoid a potential disaster.

He was later given a medal for his courage, which he typically set aside in a closet without much fanfare.

"Someone had to do it," was about all I recall him saying.

That is how I prefer to solve problems as well, one step at a time.

My friends have always told me that I am a unique problem-solver. They have praised me for my ability to research and draw conclusions based on sound methodology, experience, and reason.

The pain that shot me awake that fall morning was certainly an unpleasant way to begin the day, but its true significance was not apparent to me yet. In reality, it was the opening salvo in a fight that would last for years.

I had never experienced that kind of piercing pain, which focused like a laser on the left side of my face below my left ear.

There are, of course, benefits to being a physician. And as my head cleared itself, I soon realized it was not an ear infection because of the way the pain radiated. I knew also it was not a migraine, from which I suffered on rare occasions. It was an unfamiliar and puzzling pain whose origin or cause I could not decipher.

My first step was to take some Advil, but that did nothing, as my discomfort ramped up. So I went downstairs to my office and took some prescription Tylenol with codeine. That did nothing either.

Not wanting to disturb my wife with my agitated tossing and turning, I went down to our guest room and at some point finally fell asleep. I would do that sometimes if I was under the weather and thought I might disturb Fauzia's sleep.

When I awoke a few hours later, I thought everything was fine.

But that would soon change.

At that point, no one was looking for signs of facial paralysis.

I did notice as my head rid itself of the morning's fog that my left eye felt a little irritated, but I thought whatever and moved into the rest of the weekend calmly.

"We'll see what happens," I thought.

Monday I still had an uncomfortable feeling in my eye, as if a grain of sand had caught itself under my eyelid, so I went to see a local ophthalmologist. After an examination, he told me my left eye was extremely dry, a condition known as *keratitis sicca* or "dry cornea." It was at that point that my questions and my journey began. "Why such dryness in the left eye when my right eye is fine?" I asked. He had no answer and suggested that I see a cornea specialist the next day. The specialist was the first to notice something that no one else had seen.

After placing my chin on a rest that allowed him to study both of my eyes, he asked me to blink.

"Blink please," he said.

I thought I did.

"Blink again."

I thought I did.

"Dr. Iqbal, you are not blinking. Did you not know that?"

"Really?"

"There is some facial paralysis here."

My next step was a visit to a neurologist.

He noticed something that had been so subtle no one else had seen it.

"Your left eye is more open than your right eye," he told me.

By the time of that visit, it was becoming clear that I did indeed have some face paralysis. It was minimal but progressing ever so slowly. I was not able to blink, my left eye was not closing, and I couldn't wrinkle my forehead on the left side of my face. Yet the rest of my face appeared quite normal.

Then came the diagnosis that would stubbornly hold on through more examinations, more studies, more tests, and—illogically—more signs of what it was not.

"Maybe you have a mild case of Bell's palsy," he told me.

I must admit the diagnosis did match certain symptoms that would indeed indicate Bell's palsy, a condition that affects some forty-thousand Americans each year. But other things did not match, and as events progressed, that lack of congruency began to concern me. Yet no one else seemed to notice. It did not add up. Two plus two appeared to equal five in the views of many specialists I consulted for my facial paralysis.

Inertia is the tendency of a body in motion to continue in motion. The Bell's palsy diagnosis had taken on inertia and was coursing forward, picking up speed that my increasing doubts could not slow.

Bell's palsy is a temporary facial paralysis resulting from inflammation of the facial nerves and is often thought to be caused by a virus of some sort. One of those nerves travels through a narrow, bony canal in the skull behind the ear to the muscles on each side of the face. For most of its journey, the nerve is encased in this shell. Each facial nerve directs the muscles on one side of the face, including those that control eye blinking and closing and facial expressions, such as smiling and frowning.

The facial nerve also carries impulses to the tear and saliva glands and to the muscles of a small bone in the middle ear cavity. The facial nerve transmits taste sensations from the tongue.

Symptoms of Bell's palsy can vary from person to person. One person might have only mild weakness while others might have a range in severity from mild weakness to total paralysis. These symptoms might include twitching, weakness, or paralysis on one or, rarely, both sides of the face. Other symptoms might include drooping of the eyelid and corner of the mouth, drooling, dryness of the eye or mouth, impairment of taste, and excessive tearing in one eye.

You've likely noticed others with Bell's palsy, which is typically characterized by drooping, sagging facial skin, which at times gives those afflicted an almost grotesque-looking face.

These symptoms, which usually begin suddenly, often reach their peak within forty-eight hours. After that, the paralysis does not worsen and begins to improve in a couple of weeks.

I had some but not all of these symptoms, which complicated the diagnosis. So an initial Bell's diagnosis would make some sense. But the crucial thing about Bell's palsy is that 90 percent of the time, it goes away by itself. My symptoms never did in the eight months I labored under the diagnosis.

Facial paralysis can be caused by many conditions. Bell's palsy, while the most common one, is not the only cause.

I had a paralysis of a part of my face indeed, but it was not the kind typically seen in Bell's palsy. Despite my objections, it continued to be the verdict of every expert.

The dryness in my left eye was unrelenting and painful. Facial paralysis can interrupt the eyelid's natural blinking ability, leaving the eye dry and exposed to irritation. It's important to keep the eye moist and protect it from debris and injury, especially at night. Lubricating eye drops, ointments or gels, and eye patches can sometimes work, so I tried them all. My eyes would get terribly dry, irritated, and inflamed even though I could produce tears normally. Blinking, much like a car's windshield wiper, spreads tears across the eyeball. But because I could not blink, my tears would simply flow from my eye without actually lubricating it.

I tried a number of things to protect my eyes and went reluctantly along with the Bell's diagnosis, waiting patiently for things to clear up. Doctors and specialists know empirically what they are doing, right?

My attempts to gain some comfort included patching my left eye, but I lost depth perception and nearly crashed my car the first and only time I tried to drive with the patch.

I tried swimming goggles, which worked for the dryness but not for my near-sightedness. I found prescription goggles, but they fogged up after ten minutes. At night, I would apply gel to my eyes and tape my lids shut.

At work, I'd have to remove the goggles while seeing patients, of course. I knew I would inspire something less than confidence in my young patients and their parents looking as if I had just stepped from the pool. I replaced them with a single eye patch. Sure, I looked like a pirate, but to my little friends, that was a cool and fun look. So I began stocking pirate stickers for my patients.

When onlookers would ask what was going on with my eye, I would tell them I had scratched my cornea. The real answer would be too lengthy.

Things became ridiculously complicated.

Out of desperation, I even tried acupuncture.

Of course, it did not help. But, at that point, I would have thrown mud on my face if it would have made a difference.

I took a trip across the Hudson into New York City to get an opinion from the prestigious New York Eye and Ear Infirmary about a procedure in which surgeons would implant a thin layer of gold in my eyelid. I was told the implant was the only option to make my eye blink. I did consider it, but after more research on my own, I decided to pass in favor of a newer, more precise technique developed by Dr. Robert Levine in California.

A few months later, I flew to Los Angeles to see Dr. Levine, who implanted a metal spring in my left upper eyelid, which restored the blink to near normal levels.

In late June 2001, I awoke, startled, with the same excruciating pain around my left ear that had started the troubling journey eight months before. It was severe enough to once again take Tylenol with codeine. This time, I ran to the emergency room because my facial paralysis had suddenly worsened too.

"You've had a second attack of Bell's," my neurologist told me, prescribing some antiviral medicine and steroids.

"How often have you seen second attacks?" I asked.

"They are not common," he admitted. "I think you have had a relapse of Bell's palsy."

"How could I have a relapse if there was never a remission?" I wondered.

I underwent a very detailed examination and was subjected to an exhaustive series of tests at Columbia Presbyterian Medical Center in New York City. The doctors found nothing definitive, which in turn kept the Bell's diagnosis in play.

This cemented my growing doubts about a Bell's diagnosis, which by that time were quite strong. It made no sense; nothing added up. Something else was going on, and this opinion was seconded by a good friend, Nawed Majid, a thoracic surgeon.

"This does not sound like a second attack or relapse. What you have is a progression of the same condition."

"Exactly!" I said. "And Bell's palsy is not a progressive disease, so it cannot be Bell's." We both agreed.

The problem was that we had no alternative diagnosis.

By that time, I had completed the entire and predictable array of tests—multiple MRIs, an MRA (magnetic resonance arteriogram), blood tests, more specialists, and more tests. It was all very thorough and complete, and all those tests showed nothing at all.

This, of course, meant that the diagnostic inertia pointing to Bell's palsy continued. We don't know exactly what the problem is, so it is Bell's.

I was by that time frustrated, extremely frustrated. I knew something else was going on; my paralysis was worsening, and eight months of consults and tests had done nothing to ease that frustration.

For an unworried man, I was becoming very worried.

A number of things did not add up, and as I am wont to do, I began to study the problem myself. In effect, I had taken my own case.

When the facial nerve emerges from the skull directly underneath and slightly behind the ear, it travels between the two layers of the parotid gland. That would be crucial later in my pursuit of an answer. Facial nerves extending through the parotid gland look much like the human hand, with five extending branches, like five fingers: one to the forehead, a second to the eyes, a third to the cheekbone and nose, a fourth to the lips and mouth, and a fifth that runs underneath the jaw.

Bell's is known as a static condition, and my so-called "second attack" was strong evidence that whatever was going on, it was not static.

In July 2002, fortune smiled a bit on me. A good friend's son was getting married in Los Angeles and I was invited. Los Angeles is home to a famous clinic that was considered the country's foremost leader in the study of facial nerve disorders. In fact, researchers there had developed a grading scale used widely by physicians for gauging and measuring facial paralysis.

I would combine my joyful trip to the wedding with my more pedestrian search to find out what exactly was wrong once and for all. And once I knew what was going on, I could finally move on after these many months to getting the proper treatment.

If anyone would be able to resolve the problem, it would be the experts at that clinic.

They would know.

I was enormously hopeful and buoyed, and so with my CT scans and MRIs tucked firmly under my arms, I got on a plane and headed to the wedding in Los Angeles.

After a wonderful reunion with my friends at the wedding, it was time to get down to business. A physician who had read my reports and reviewed my forms greeted me at the clinic. He listened to my history, reviewed my scans, and immediately dropped the bombshell.

"Dr. Iqbal, you have had a second attack of Bell's palsy, and it is likely permanent."

I was stunned.

He continued, "Luckily for you, we still have an extremely narrow window of opportunity to correct it. I highly recommend that you cancel your plans to return to New Jersey tomorrow and let us do something for you."

That "something" was a procedure called middle fossa decompression of the facial nerve, in which surgeons would cut—somewhat urgently, it appeared by his tone that morning—into my skull, lift my brain out of the way, and destroy the bone around the facial nerve to release pressure.

"This is your only hope," he told me.

I was completely unprepared for such drastic advice and sat still, speechless, dumbfounded. What do I do now? What *should* I do?

CHAPTER 3
A FAVORED CHILD

I knew that in their eyes, I was my large family's sweet baby, meant to be pampered and cared for and kept safe. That was all that mattered to me.

My four brothers and my sister doted on me and showered me with affection. They protected me and gave me a sense of security that I now realize provided me with the idea that I could overcome any obstacle. They showed me a world in which there were no barriers or problems—only love.

My extended family, including my grandparents and uncles, had among them pioneers who lived during what I imagine would be the Punjabi version of the Wild West, with great perilous treks and horseback kidnappings, humbling poverty, and the pure snobbery that only life in the British Raj can engender. One of my grandmothers had firsthand contact with the upper crust of British society in India during her childhood. My other grandmother came from humble beginnings but rose to such prominence that the entire region mourned her death ninety years later.

As a young boy, I knew none of this, of course. I knew only the security of my immediate family's protection.

When I was ten, I visited the home of my maternal grandmother in Gojra, now a bustling city of more than 100,000 residents near Faisalabad in north-central Pakistan. When I visited there in the late 1950s, it seemed to be a small and rather inconsequential town. I was unimpressed as only a bored ten-year-old would be, curious only about an incongruously sunken park the size of the soccer field located across the street from my family home. I should have been more curious.

Gojra was established in 1896, and Chirag Deen, my grandfather, was instrumental in creating it. The story of how he came to Gojra and how a large ugly hole in the ground became a manicured park with gently descending steps and neatly trimmed hedges would later turn my adolescent disinterest into overflowing pride. His story of migration is similar to those of other migrants anywhere in the world. I learned of our family farm and how a growing number of siblings waited for a plot of land that was becoming increasingly smaller, sliced like a shrinking pie. The practice was unsustainable, and at some point, something had to give. The writing was on the wall, and my grandfather could read it clearly.

So at age twenty, he was smart and ambitious enough in the late 1800s to see a tempting bit of light in British plans to entice settlers out into the hostile and arid hinterland of the southwestern Punjab. Irrigate and they will come, they believed. The British began building a system of canals that would provide water and irrigation and a chance for land.

My grandfather jumped at the chance to own his own land, and with a dozen or so other brave souls, he set off on an arduous three-hundred-mile, month long trek from the security of Sialkot into an alien land. It was a land populated by cobras, scorpions, and notorious dacoits, feral and infamous bandits who were no strangers to a casual throat-slitting or head-bashing if it suited them. Everything he needed was tucked in a carefully folded cotton sheet tied to the end of a *dang*, a long metal-tipped wooden rod that could prove useful for many things, including warding off wild animals, crushing snakes and scorpions, and perhaps stunning the rare bird or rabbit for dinner.

Inside his makeshift bag, tied to his dang, my grandfather kept flour and a vial of oil and onions that he and his companions would cook each night over a fire lit from the rare scavenged branches and twigs, set in a small hole to protect it from the winds of the open Punjab. A lot of these details have been lost in the retelling of that trek and now, from the secure confines of my own comfortable home in New Jersey, I wonder if they had milk, if they ever went without food, if they were able to kill an occasional animal, or if they were ever confronted by dacoits. I have my suspicions.

Eventually, the intrepid group would reach what is now Gojra, though no one in my family knows exactly why they chose that destination. My guess is that it was close to a new canal and seemed the right place for a farming community. Perhaps they were simply exhausted.

The new settlers' first order of business was to build shelter, and they commenced digging, fashioning adobe bricks from the hard clay of their new settlement, from which they built their homes. Flash forward 120 years, and today from the comfort of one's own home via laptop, one can click on Google Earth and see the homes they built, still standing in a neat, perfect row in Gojra. I have to admit it is quite impressive. However, the result of that flurry of construction and all that digging up of soil to make bricks was a deep, ugly hole that was quite an eyesore.

My grandfather became the de facto leader of the pilgrims during the long trek, and he did not like the hole, so he decided to use it to celebrate the difficult journey and their new home. "Let's make this a nice park," he said. And so they did. When I visited there as that unimpressed kid, I walked down ten feet of steps to reach that park, which was now lush green and surrounded by a fence. Its serenity masked the intense effort it took to create it years before.

Over the ensuing years, my grandfather would become the *pinsal nawees*—in effect, the mayor—of the growing village. He was the public official charged with communicating with the British authorities to ensure each farmer received the right amount of water from the widening system of canals.

Another bit of a family lore relates this story. One day, the villagers, terrorized by a menacing cobra in the center of town, had shut themselves in, scared out of their wits. My grandfather, it is said, took care of things. Walking into the center of town with his *dang*, he told the cobra, "Listen, in this village, there can be only one person everyone fears, and that happens to be me." With that, he crushed the cobra's head.

As the residents of Gojra settled, the town grew, and my grandfather's role as *pinsal nawees* solidified, he noticed a local shopkeeper and how he kept his young teenage daughter with him during the day. It seems the man's wife had died, and he didn't know what to do with his daughter. Frontier towns being what frontier towns are, he was reluctant to leave his daughter alone and did not trust anyone enough to care for her.

So that day and every day, right there in his clothing shop, the father began teaching his daughter through reading the Quran to her. Then he expanded the lessons to Urdu, Arabic, math, geography, and history. Each day was a tremendous learning experience for the young girl, and she seemed to absorb everything in the merchant's makeshift classroom quickly.

A few years passed, and Gojra grew and began taking on the semblance of a real and flourishing town. Perhaps it was time to establish a school for the steadily growing population of girls, the British thought. Culture and tradition dictated that the teacher must be female too. The problem, however, was that there was not a single educated woman in the entire area.

This dilemma caught the attention of the shopkeeper. His daughter was fully educated and qualified for the job, but she was too young and had no diploma. He approached the British authorities and requested that, in lieu of the diploma, this young "woman" should be allowed to take an exam to prove her qualification.

On the day of the exam, he dressed his thirteen-year-old daughter in the traditional women's head-to-toe -covering, the burka. He added to her height by having her step into high-heeled shoes. Then he escorted her to the exam.

She passed easily. In fact, she scored higher than anyone's expectations. At thirteen, she became Gojra's first school teacher. Later, as the school expanded, she became its first headmistress.

A few years later, she would also become my grandmother, Chirag Bibi. Later, she would give birth to my mother, Kulsoom.

Over the years as a teacher in Gojra, she became a leading and much-beloved citizen—a saint, many people would say. When she died at age ninety in 1960, it seemed almost the entire city of Gojra, many of whose citizens she had taught, mourned her death and attended her funeral.

My father's mother was of an entirely different stripe. Zorha Jaan was a spoiled princess who believed the world and everyone in it owed her a living. Like the members of the high British society she grew up with, she had an almost disdainful view of everyone who did not shower her with what she believed was her rightful benediction.

Zohra Jaan felt entitled her entire life, an attitude that would bear sour fruit later. Her abusive treatment of my mother prompted my family to move from my grandparents' home long before I was born.

Zohra Jaan's kidnapping by my father's father, a rakishly handsome and clearly adventurous young man, would provide another source of family legend. Sixty years later, it still sparked arguments among the participants.

It all started when my grandfather Siraj Deen swept her off her feet in a Punjabi version of *Romeo and Juliet*. Zohra came from a wealthy and influential family, and she was raised in the household of Lord George Nathaniel Curzon, British viceroy and governor-general of India from 1898 to 1905. Zohra's father was Lord Curzon's tutor in Urdu and Indian customs and a frequent visitor to the viceregal palace, usually with adorable little Zohra in tow. The viceroy had three little daughters of his own, about the same age as Zohra, and before long, they all became inseparable friends.

Whatever his historical reputation had been for fierceness, arrogance, and stubbornness, according to Zohra, Lord Curzon was apparently a very human man, often playfully carrying her around on his shoulders. She would later recount her brushes with such greatness—as if it were a trait both contagious and inherited—in full detail.

With her peachy-cream complexion, long and flowing reddish hair, and hazel eyes, Zohra was by all accounts (her own included) a much-sought-after and beautiful young woman. As was the custom, she was a highly coveted prize and was married at age sixteen to a young man from a prominent Indian family.

But her golden life was short-lived. Her husband died six months later, leaving her in many ways a captive of his family, who essentially controlled her life. It was, according to custom, unlikely she would ever marry again, a widow at sixteen, bound somehow by custom and honor to remain faithful to her dead husband and the wishes of his family.

That was until she met Siraj Deen.

Siraj Deen was the youngest brother of my maternal grandfather Chirag and, as family legend recounts, a bit of a rogue. When he met Zohra by chance one day, they were both struck down and bowled over, deeply in love immediately.

He would marry this princess, but he had to overcome one small detail. If they did marry, he would likely be killed by her angry and dishonored former in-laws. The wedding ceremony would have to be quiet, and it would have to take place quickly and surreptitiously, after which Siraj could spirit her away back to Sialkot when it would be too late for the aggrieved in-laws to interfere.

Eventually, they came up with a plan. Siraj and his small wedding party would venture to Zohra's village armed and on horseback, where they would be married quickly and without fanfare. Celebrations would take place more safely in Sialkot.

They knew it was unlikely that they would pull off the surprise wedding and get away before the angry former in-laws found out, and they knew even if they did, there would be a fight and a chase. Family lore has it that another of Siraj's bothers, Saed, volunteered to stay behind and fend off the in-laws.

It almost worked. As they were leaving an impromptu ceremony, the wedding party noticed a dozen or more men armed with dangs approaching rapidly on horseback. Hurriedly, the groom jumped up on his horse, hoisted his new bride up with one arm, and sped away toward Sialkot. Saed did as he promised and stood in the angry relatives' path, challenging them to a fight while the wedding party fled. Grossly outnumbered and outmatched, he sustained serious injuries. Yet he fought long enough to allow Siraj and Zohra to make it back to Sialkot safely.

Saed never let my grandfather forget his efforts, even years later, chastising him when there was an argument. "Don't ever raise your voice, to me," he would say to my grandfather. "I saved your butt."

A very tall and muscular man of legendary strength and bravery, Saed had an epiphany in his later years. He gave up all his worldly possessions and devoted his life to God. He would travel from village to village, carrying just a shoulder bag filled with religious books, preaching to anyone and everyone he met.

Siraj and Zohra would become the parents of my father, Mohammed Iqbal.

In later years, Zohra was a terror. As was the custom, my father and his growing family lived with his parents in Sialkot while he worked his way up the hierarchy of the railroad. This, of course, meant he would have to spend long stretches of time away from us, attending to his career. While he was away, Zohra treated my mother as if she were an indentured servant. My mother, with two young children, toiled all day with chores, cooking, cleaning, and washing all the while putting up with her mother-in-law's relentless verbal and occasional physical abuse.

My mother said nothing, never fought back, and never complained to her husband. Then one day, he walked in unexpectedly and saw Zohra dump a pot of boiling hot soup at my mother's feet.

They moved out soon after.

This all happened long before I was born. My childhood was quiet and comforting and allowed me to pursue my love for books and learning. While my older brothers and sister would be charged each day with a chore, I was freed from such tedium. The young prince that I was, I never did a single thing that could be described as menial work. To this day, I cannot even hang a picture or drill a hole in the wall. Such was my life of ease. Everyone spoiled me. I never even went shopping until I came to the United States some twenty years later, and when I did, I didn't know even the basics of choosing a piece of meat or how to tell if fruit was ripe and good to buy. The pleasant bubble in which I lived was comforting and serene, and I did not complain.

The love my brothers and sister and I had for each other, our sense of family, and how we treated each other would show themselves many years later, after both my parents had died. When my father died in January 1976, my brother Mansoor became the family executor and he transferred all my father's assets to our mother. When she passed away in 1998, we fought among ourselves, which is not unusual when an estate is in question and children line up, so to speak, to inherit some long-awaited rewards for their family devotions.

Our family fight over legacies and inheritances was different though. We fought to give our shares to the others. Javed and I, being the most well off, decided to give most of our shares to our other three brothers. That was when each one of them called us, individually and privately, to make a case that the other two brothers were more deserving than they. Each one wanted the others to have a bigger share. I think this sort of unique selflessness is because of the way we were all raised, and the highest honor belongs to our parents.

Children learn by watching. We watched our parents love and cherish their parents and siblings and make sacrifices for them. We watched and we learned, just as our children are watching and learning from us.

I still cherish memories of my father rising early to set the household wheels in motion on winter mornings, starting fires to ward off the chills and warming the house before we all awoke. If he had time, he would take a break to come into my room and snuggle with me beneath the covers under the warmth of a pile comforting quilts. Often he would tell me adventure stories and sing to me in his beautiful soothing voice, sometimes reciting verses from the Quran or Urdu poetry. These are comforting thoughts now, even sixty years later.

In a family of boys, my sister was a prize jewel for my parents, the darling daughter they cherished and adored. We would lose Zahida much too early when she died at age thirty-three, but when she was a child and a young woman, my parents put her in a special place. She was worshipped by her brothers as well, because she had a gift few people have. When she spoke to you and was with you, you felt that she loved you alone more than anyone. When I was with her, I felt no one else in the entire world existed but the two of us.

Even so, she and my brother Mansoor had a special, indefinable love for each other that showed itself in many ways that are hard to describe unless you had seen them together. It was a special bond.

Mansoor today, at age eighty two, is now our family patriarch, but at one point when I was quite young, he was a first-year college student with a two-hour-long daily commute to Lahore. Some of my first memories are of Mansoor rising at some ungodly hour to get to the train. But no matter when he awoke, Zahida, only thirteen years old, was already up, gathering wood, lighting fires for the stove, and preparing his breakfast and packing him a lunch. I can still see her holding out her hand to give Mansoor the parathas, chapatis, and omelets she had cooked for him before he awoke.

We all loved Zahida, and the lengths to which my parents went to show it were extraordinary.

When I was ten years old, she got married, a singular event in any family, but in ours, for my parents, it was extraordinary.

My father, a man of great pride, was someone who kept his emotions in check in public. But at Zahida's wedding, he made an emphatic point at the celebration, which was teeming with hundreds of wedding guests. In front of everyone, he pulled the groom to the center of the room as he and Zahida were about to leave. He was in tears as he put his hands over his face, overcome and no longer keeping his rigid demeanor intact—no longer putting up his front. With his hands clasped in front of his face, like a beggar seeking alms, his voice quivering, he said, "Son, you must promise me you will take good care of her. Please. She is the most precious possession I have, and if she is ever unhappy, even for a second, my heart will bleed."

It was a wrenching but powerful scene, and the raucous crowd of guests fell silent.

I was beside myself as well. As Zahida was preparing to leave, she pulled me aside and hugged me tightly, kissing me, trying to dry my tears. But I was inconsolable. I was losing my beloved sister—it was like losing part of myself—and I could not understand why. I left and was found later in a storage room under a pile of blankets where I had fallen asleep. The blankets were soaked from my crying.

The enormous responsibility my parents felt for sending Zahida off properly and providing a suitable and generous dowry and sufficient amount of pomp and ceremony can be summed up fairly easily. They spent everything they had, literally.

Shortly after the wedding, as was usually the case, I came home from school with my brother Ejaz, who was two years older. We were hungry and waiting as we usually did for our mother to prepare us lunch. Usually we would be greeted upon walking into the kitchen by several pots simmering on the stove, our noses welcomed by a wonderful mix of spices and enticing smells, all conjured up by our mother. But not that day.

In our mother's nervous eyes, we saw she had nothing. There were no simmering pots and no spread of things into which we could dive. Our parents were broke to the point that they had no food.

Instead, we saw that she had sliced up some potatoes, just potatoes that usually served only as a base for other delights—no meat, no fish, no greens, no lentils. There was not even ghee in which to cook those lowly potatoes. Instead, our mother had pulled out some mustard oil, which was normally used as a hair preparation and certainly not for cooking. She was mortified but had nothing else to offer. She reluctantly, tearfully, served us our lunch.

Today, I'd tell you my mother had cooked us French fries, even though she did not know it. We loved them and thought they were a special and exotic treat we had never eaten before. They were outrageously delicious.

Our verdict on the new delicacy our mother had been so reluctant and embarrassed to cook for us? "Can you please cook these for us every day?"

She hugged us in tears. "Thank you," she said to us, bewildered. "Thank you."

Such was life in the Iqbal family. Things went on as they did, and we never worried about too much, even a lack of money.

I still carry that gentle, unhurried philosophy forward in my life today, cancer or not, stress or not, pain or not. One creates one's own world, I think. It can be harsh and unforgiving and unwarranted and cruel, or it can be smooth. It's up to us.

I truly believe people have much control over how they view things. We rarely have any power over what happens in our lives. How we deal with adversity is always up to us.

As I grew older, my only concern was my schoolwork, which drew me in from the beginning, captured me, really, and at which I excelled, to the point where I would become upset if I was not first in my class.

I pursued my schoolwork and earned high marks and class ranking, which I carried with an air of quiet confidence. I never strutted or postured, and I was never arrogant.

My father would never have approved of arrogance or cockiness in any form from me or my brothers, just as he would have been appalled at any of us doing anything colored even slightly with a taint of dishonesty. Along with his work ethic, this was something he passed on to us all. "Honesty is in our blood," he would say. "You will never succeed if you're dishonest."

While I was pursuing my schoolboy quest for first-in-class honors, I also began to realize the importance of occasionally lifting my head from the textbooks, of widening my interests a bit.

I pursued a strong interest in debating and was thrilled to participate; I enjoyed writing and at fourteen began a

weekly column for our local newspaper, pointing out the social injustice of various community events. I did this under a
pseudonym, because no reader would believe such pointed
and opinionated writing would be coming from a teenager.
The column became quite popular, but few people outside
of the newspaper editor and I knew who the writer was. Not
even my mother or brothers knew. It was heady stuff for a
young kid.

My passion for debating grew as I did. I relished being
able to make a point and to win. My brother Ejaz was also
into debating and was exceptionally good at it. More often
than not, we found ourselves on the opposite sides of the
aisle, engaging in spirited arguments and debating point-
counterpoint. We drew energy from each other, and together we won lots of trophies.

One constant in all this was my father, who relished every minute of it and attended as many of these productions
as he could, proudly watching from the front row.

All these activities and the attention they brought me
never diverted me from the one goal I had had since I could
remember. I wanted to be a doctor. That was a blessing,
and knowing that so early, knowing what I wanted to do at
so young an age, allowed me to focus. I have always been
focused. It helped me then, and it helped during my cancer
struggle. Even my siblings and parents joked about it, call-
ing me "doctor" even when I was in elementary school.

I was not alone in wanting a career in medicine. My
brother Javed went before me and in a way paved the path
for me as good older brothers do sometimes. Today he also
lives in New Jersey, a highly regarded psychiatrist. After his
own lengthy studies and residencies in the United States

and Scotland, he went back to Pakistan, but he quickly realized that the Pakistani medical community was combative, backstabbing, jealous, and parochial. It was not an environment in which one flourished. Javed's observations and experiences as a young psychiatrist in Karachi would later come into play in my own life and career.

After high school, I was accepted to a premed course in the Punjabi city of Bahawalpur, my first step in a long journey to my goal. The standard path at the time called for students who did well in premed courses to apply to a medical school after two years. It was the beginning of the winnowing process. In my own world, with the, I guess, almost blind confidence that came from excelling in high school, I did not even invest a heartbeat of a thought about how competitive such an arrangement was. When I finished my premed courses, I applied to medical school and was accepted. I would learn later that only two of us from that premed class of one hundred actually got into medical school.

I breezed through, though, and at age seventeen in 1964, I was a medical school student beginning the first of five years at Nishtar Medical College in Multan. That first year was an eye-opener for me.

As I made my way through classes that first year, I thought, "So, what's the big deal?" I studied as I always had, which is to say I did enough but not more. That had always pulled me to the first position in my class in grammar school and high school, and it had been sufficient to get me through my premed course. I was fortunate that things had always come naturally to me.

I was rudely awakened from that conceit at the end of my first year at Nishtar, though. When examination results were announced, I saw that I had passed, to be sure, but just barely. I was not at the top of my class for the first time but rather just barely over the passing mark. My two roommates and lifelong friends, Javaid and Mehboob, had scored poorly too. We had all been tops of our classes, but that first year, we found ourselves in a group of about 130 medical students who had all been tops in their classes. We were no longer the golden boys but rather part of the herd. We were not unique, and we had fallen into some bad habits that first year. That, to me and my roommates, was a wake-up call.

We all looked at each other after the results came out and, chagrined, said, "We have to study harder." And for the next four years, we did.

But I also had a bit of an epiphany about the need to have a rounded experience, not simply bury myself into my books to the point that I was not aware that life was going on outside Nishtar. I would not become a hermit, I decided. I would do well in school to be sure, but I would live life as well.

Beginning my second year, I made a conscious decision to pay attention to my other passions. I was still fond of literature, so I wrote poetry and short stories and became the editor of Nishtar's literary magazine. I joined the debate team and acted in school plays. I no longer felt the unabated urge to be number one. I wanted to do well, but I wanted to live well also.

A photo I still have of the college cricket team from 1968 is a perfect example. I'm there in the back row in the official team photo, all eleven of us turned out in our best cricket whites. I enjoyed sports but was far from a skilled athlete; however, I traveled with the teams as the official scorer and loved the camaraderie it brought. It earned me a spot in the photo.

Years later, when he was still a young boy, Sheeraz saw the photo one day and was duly impressed, as any son would be.

"Were you the best player?" he asked.

"No, Sheeraz, I was not the best."

"Were you the second best, then?"

"No, Sheeraz, not the second either."

"Third?"

He would not give up until I told him I was likely the eleventh best on an eleven-man team. With a mix of amusement and regret, I saw a fleeting look of disappointment on my son's face before he moved on to something else.

School was the same. No longer was I driven to be the first. I was happy to keep up in the top 10 percent. It allowed me to widen my horizons.

In my last year of medical school, I realized I wanted to go into pediatrics, and when I mentioned that to my professor of pediatrics, he seemed exceptionally happy. He had been following my progress through school apparently. To my great surprise and delight, he invited me to do my pediatric residency—what we called in Pakistan a "house job"—with him when I graduated.

This was a tremendous relief. Of the 130 members of my class, only about twenty-five would qualify for the paid "house jobs." The rest would have to make do with unpaid residencies.

That professor, Shaukat Raza Khan, became a wonderful, thoughtful, and generous teacher, and I grew to love him as I worked and learned under him in Multan. House jobs were designed to prepare future doctors for postgraduate certification following a rigorous exam that was the final step to being a specialist. Students who passed the exam would be accorded the lofty title of MCPS, Member of the Pakistan College of Physicians and Surgeons. Residents usually sat for the MCPS only after honing their skills and sharpening their practical knowledge for sometimes as many as five years. Again, I felt honored and thrilled to hear my mentor announce when I was only a year into my house job that I was ready for the MCPS exam. It was a fulfilling compliment from him.

By this time, my brother Javed was back in Pakistan after distinguishing himself during his postgraduate work in the United States and Scotland. The medical hierarchy in Karachi and its petty jealousies disillusioned him. It was difficult under the circumstances for him to even attempt to make a name for himself in Karachi, and he was planning to pursue an offer from the University of Medicine and Dentistry in New Jersey.

I spoke with Javed after I learned of my chance to sit for the MCPS and become a specialist in record time.

"Why?" he asked.

"Because it will allow me to become a specialist in Pakistan almost immediately after my house job," I told him, feeling quite disappointed at his obvious lack of awe. Again, he asked why, telling me I should instead apply for a pediatric residency in the United States.

I had never given that prospect too much thought. A number of my medical school friends had done US residencies at various times, but I had never seriously entertained the idea of more training in the States. I enjoyed my status in Pakistan. And I loved being near my family and friends. It was a sweet, wonderfully optimistic time in my life.

But at Javed's urging, I decided to give it a try, though I did so almost halfheartedly. In fact, a friend had a number of unused applications to various American programs, and I simply used two of those without much care. The only thing I knew was that if I was going to the United States, it would be somewhere in New York City. I wanted to be at the heart of it all.

So in October 1970, I applied to programs at two hospitals in New York City. My thought at the time was that if I was accepted, I would not have to make a decision for six months, when most programs opened, which would have been July 1971.

Then my blissful procrastination came to a crashing halt. Two weeks after my halfhearted application, an offer came back, and it even included a contract to sign along with a promise of a free airline ticket to New York City. If I was willing, there was an opening at the New York Infirmary, but I would have to get there by January 1.

"You have exactly what we are looking for," the letter read.

I was flattered, but now I had to make a decision. I turned again to Javed. I can still clearly recall hopping on my bicycle and the sunny ride into the center of Multan to a bank of phones at the telegraph office, which provided the long-distance lines I needed to reach him in Karachi.

I explained the situation to Javed: the surprise offer, the need to leave almost immediately, the effect it would have on my plans for the MCPS exam, and my reluctance to leave home—the details of my procrastination unraveling on the telegraph office floor as I spoke.

"I need more time," I told Javed. "I need your advice. What should I do?"

Javed was abrupt, quick, and to the point, as he often is. "Go," he said.

CHAPTER 4

THE BATTLE BEGINS

July 2001

A chance encounter with a former classmate half a world and decades away from my days in Pakistan would shift my focus to a place where it should have been all along. After my brief glow of optimism about finding an answer to my troubling facial paralysis was snuffed out at the famous clinic, I began to wonder how I would contest the growing number of physicians who continued to insist I had Bell's palsy.

It is said that the definition of insanity is doing the same thing over and over and expecting different results. Perhaps then, I was on the brink of insanity, because for nine months, I continued to see specialists and hope one of them would do the simple arithmetic and recognize that whatever was troubling me was not Bell's.

From where I sat on the outside of that special circle of experts, I began to look at medical specialists and their exalted station in the medical community and was reminded of an old Indian parable.

Medical specialists are highly trained, highly qualified, and often venerated. They've had years of focused, intense education and are for the most part elevated to lofty, god-like positions—often in their own minds. But as my frustration continued to grow, my attempts to break through the auras and have a simple conversation were thwarted at every turn. I began to think of those doctors as the blind men examining an elephant. The story tells how six blind men were asked by their king to describe an elephant by feeling different parts of its body. One blind man felt a leg and said the elephant was like a pillar; the one who felt the tail said the elephant was like a rope; the one who felt the trunk said the elephant is like a tree branch; the one who felt the ear said the elephant was like a hand fan; the one who felt the belly said the elephant was like a wall; and the one who felt the tusk said the elephant was like a solid pipe.

The king told them after they were finished with their assessments that they were all correct, but they had missed the larger point. From that age-old parable one learns that while one's subjective experience can be true, it can also be severely limited. Narrow perspectives can sometimes limit the larger truth, which I suspected was the situation in my case. With their limited views, my specialists were missing the larger point.

The neurologists I consulted initially were exclusively focused on my brain, as that was their area of expertise. If they could not find a problem in my brain, then I must have Bell's palsy, they thought.

The very bright young physician I saw at Columbia Presbyterian Medical Center ran all kinds of blood tests to look for systemic medical illnesses that could have caused a nerve paralysis. Since all of those came back negative, he also concluded that I must have Bell's palsy. Of course, he too was wrong.

The famous expert at the LA clinic was so heavily involved in this rather new and exciting surgical treatment for Bell's palsy that he had developed tunnel vision. To him, every patient with facial paralysis had Bell's and needed surgery. I was quickly beginning to appreciate a very different side to the medicine I had practiced for decades. Each one of those experts was handicapped by a severe case of tunnel vision. Six blind men and an elephant!

On the flight out to Los Angeles on the Fourth of July weekend, I was calm, hopeful, and a bit excited. I felt my visit to the doctors there would finally put an end to the Bell's diagnosis, which had been my shadow for too long, despite facts that would indicate something else was at play. There is no test for Bell's, so in the face of test results that could not pinpoint any other specific problem, the Bell's diagnosis stuck with me, unfortunately.

The repeat of my October 2000 experience—the sudden excruciating pain on the left side of my face that woke me and started the whole thing going again—had been enough to send me to the ER for an injection of cortisone and antiviral drugs. And now the paralysis was increasing. "It is a relapse of Bell's," I was told. "The Bell's is progressing." I just couldn't take it anymore. The fact that Bell's is not a progressive condition did nothing to deter the various physicians I saw.

I had gone to Los Angeles with high hopes, but they were quickly and resoundingly dashed as the Bell's diagnosis continued to haunt me.

After discussing my problem and during what seemed to be only a perfunctory review of the Columbia test results, I sat across a sunlit desk from one of the well-known physicians in LA who is recognized for his knowledge of facial paralysis and its various causes. He recommended an operation called "the middle fossa facial decompression".

It was not what I had expected.

Today, the procedure is often used to treat Bell's palsy, but at the time, it was still relatively new and unfamiliar.

The facial nerve, the crucial source of so many functions, travels through a narrow, bony canal at the base of the skull. When its emerges, it passes through the parotid gland and then splits and spreads below the ear like the delta of a large river, branching out into five smaller rivulets and spreading across the face. This bony canal is nature's way of protecting the nerve. There is no free space around the facial nerve in this segment of its journey.

In theory, and as viewed by specialists, the viral infection that causes Bell's makes the facial nerve swell, and as it passes through the extremely tight space in the skull, the compression leads to a loss of function and then paralysis.

During this procedure, the doctor surgically destroys the walls of this bony canal to give the nerve some room to expand. The swelling would still be there, but after the surgery, there would be no compression, which would free the nerve to recover its function. Eventually, the virus goes away and the swelling goes down.

As mentioned earlier, the doctors in LA wanted to open my skull and push my brain aside temporarily while they destroyed the wall of the bony canal. As the surgeon calmly described the procedure sitting there across from me at his desk, it seemed relatively benign, but the thought of someone lifting my brain and pushing it aside while he drilled a hole in my skull seemed anything but benign.

Still, the theory made good sense as a treatment for Bell's palsy. However, I did not have Bell's palsy and I was positive about that. I was stunned, actually, sitting there listening to the doctor talk as if destroying the passage was no more difficult than vacuuming my living room rug. Again, the dichotomy of life on the other side of medicine was being illustrated for me, whether I liked it or not. Shock and disappointment raced through my mind as I attempted to absorb the recommendation of what seemed like a radical operation. I had problems controlling my thoughts. I had expected a quick and neat solution—a proper and accurate diagnosis. Instead, I was being led down the same disastrous path. Sitting there, reeling, I knew in my gut they were wrong. Why wouldn't anyone believe me and take a chance by thinking outside the standard medical box? Inside me, a voice was screaming, but I sat there, my usual composed self, saying a silent prayer that I hoped would be answered.

But what does one do when one of the country's leading experts insists not only on a radical procedure but also on doing it immediately or risking great peril?

"You don't have much time," he told me. "The window of opportunity to do this is closing." Would this unchallenged expert want me to argue to press my point? Should I insist he was wrong and tell him my viewpoint? Should I show him the evidence of his folly? Did I dare to question him?

"I'll think about it," I said. "But if I decide to go ahead with it, I want it done near my home. I'll have it done in New York."

He seemed fine with my decision and didn't overtly push, though he left me with these cautionary words: "Don't wait too long."

Still reeling, I returned to the hotel. It might have been Independence Day weekend, but I was still trapped inside the seemingly unbreakable hold of an erroneous and improper diagnosis perpetuated by all those experts who stubbornly refused to look beyond that. I did not feel any amount of strength in being alone in my opinion that something else was happening to me. Nothing added up, but in the arithmetic of the specialists I had seen so far, it didn't matter. When I got back to the hotel, I sought out two friends, both physicians, who had also attended the wedding. It was only two days before, but in light of the proposed surgical procedure I had just been presented with, it felt like months.

We spoke calmly and deliberatively about the situation, considered the ramifications of the suggested surgery and the likelihood that I did not have Bell's, and arrived at two courses of action. First, I would definitely not have the surgery in Los Angeles, and second, I would seek out more help from additional specialists. My friends were nothing if not efficient, and before we headed up to our rooms for the night, they had sourced the names of two physicians at two of the best medical centers in the country, Johns Hopkins and the Cleveland Clinic.

I was champing at the bit to put this entirely too long process to an end. I couldn't afford to waste any more time. We flew back to New Jersey Sunday evening, and first thing on Monday, I called and left messages for both experts. Surprisingly, they called me back quickly. But discussing my symptoms and the various and unsuccessful remedial attempts over the previous months yielded a common refrain. Neither could quickly arrive at the neat and clean solution I wanted so badly. However, both doctors shared my skepticism about the Bell's palsy diagnosis and validated my reluctance to consent to a major surgery under these circumstances. This was encouraging to some extent.

Before I would jump blindly into a surgical solution, I wanted to nail down an airtight diagnosis. Then I could proceed with what I needed to do. For me, this was nonnegotiable. I thought of the round of exhaustive tests I had undergone at Columbia Presbyterian after my second attack of extreme pain—the "recurrence" of the nonrecurring Bell's. The doctor I had seen at Columbia was a neurologist, so he was looking for some sort of neurological dysfunction that could be causing problems. The thought was—and it made sense to me—if they could find and identify a concrete indication of some pathology that could be causing the paralysis and pain and dryness—they could eliminate Bell's. But those tests found nothing. In a way, it was addition by subtraction, a process of elimination. All the tests came back negative for something other than Bell's, so it must be Bell's. Infuriating!

It was the blind men and the elephant. It was tunnel vision and pretzel logic, a specialty of those specialists, I was learning.

So, we proved that there was nothing wrong with my brain. The problem had to be somewhere else. But where?

Now back home, my disappointment with the famous clinic and the lack of epiphanies from the specialists at Hopkins and Cleveland Clinic were beginning to set deep roots. I called Columbia again and spoke with another specialist. I updated him on my various quests for answers and the recommendation for surgery. I recounted my frustration and the need for an accurate diagnosis so I could finally seek a proper treatment.

He assured me that if surgery was necessary—and he wasn't ruling it out—it could be done in New York. This Columbia physician was a highly regarded neurotologist, trained in disorders of the ear, specifically how various conditions can affect the nerves in and around the ear, which was where my problems seemed to be originating.

My thinking by this time—and I'm not certain if I was simply goaded by my frustration for action, *any* kind of action—was that he would be the best person to help me realize my search for an answer. I asked for an appointment to see him as quickly as possible. He could see me in two weeks, he said. Cautiously, I started to hope again.

If I hired an actuary to calculate the odds of me meeting a former medical school classmate from Multan in a crowded wedding hall in South Jersey, to be serendipitously assigned a seat right next to him at the reception, that actuary would be severely challenged. And if I then asked that actuary to further calculate the odds that my former classmate would provide me with a gift that would help solve my medical dilemma, he would blow a fuse.

It comes down to one simple premise: *People come into your life for a reason.*

In mid-July, Fauzia and I found ourselves at a crowded wedding reception in southern New Jersey near Philadelphia. When we reached our assigned table and sat down, I noticed one of the gentlemen seated across from us give a sudden start, his head snapping back a bit in some sort of recognition.

"Sajjad?" he asked, the beginning of a smile crossing his face. "My God."

I looked across the table and in slow-motion focus recognized a former medical school classmate, Munir.

"Munir?" I said, just as visibly startled as he was.

We had not seen each other since 1969, when we graduated and went our separate ways from school in Multan, Pakistan. To be sitting across from him at a table in New Jersey hard off the busy traffic and uninterrupted noise of Interstate 95 was, to say the least, an amazing coincidence.

Munir had not been a close friend at school, but of course the conversation quickly became nostalgic and wistful as we recalled days long past in our home country so far away from that New Jersey wedding banquet hall. It was a wonderful surprise.

Munir told me he was an associate professor of gynecology at a university in Philadelphia. I proudly told him of my family and my pediatric practice. The conversation, of course, eventually swung to my facial paralysis and the inability of my doctors to find a proper diagnosis. I told him of my struggle with the specialists to get them to see that I did not have Bell's. I gave him the entire and painful blow-by-blow account of how I had been disappointed by some of the most highly regarded specialists in the country.

"I know it is not Bell's," I said. "I wish they could tell me what it is."

Munir leaned in, pushing aside his dessert plate. "You know, Sajjad, the fault is yours, not theirs. Don't blame them."

"Mine?" I replied. "Are you crazy? How do you come to that conclusion?"

He looked at me calmly, this middle-aged doctor I had not seen in more than thirty years who had just popped into my life again.

"Because you are putting your faith in other people when it is in your power to find the answer," he said. "You are capable of finding the answer yourself," he added for emphasis. "Are these doctors smarter than you?"

"Munir," I replied, "the point is, this is not my area of specialty and I know much less about this subject than they do. After all, they are the experts in this field."

He looked at me in what I can describe only as disbelief. Then he explained to me that when we were in medical school together, he had thought of me as one of the top-tier students. "I always admired you for that," he said. "We were all impressed at how smart you were. I always thought you knew everything we didn't know."

"What happened to that Sajjad?" he continued. "Do you think these specialists, these so-called experts, are now smarter than you? I find that unlikely," he reminded me.

I was buoyed by his reminiscences, of course, and flattered. But I was still leery. It had been a long nine months, and I was growing exhausted. Later, I would learn what real exhaustion truly felt like.

"But, Munir, the point is, they are the specialists in this field and I am not. How do I go about finding a diagnosis?"

Munir was unmoved. "I don't know, but you'll figure it out…if you put your mind to it."

That was the end of our conversation. I have not seen Munir or talked to him since. It was as if an angel had crossed my path that night at just the right time when I had begun to lose faith.

Munir's admonitions and vote of confidence allowed me to transfer the faith I had been putting in those specialists to myself. But how was I going to pull it off? It would have been easy to dismiss Munir and simply wait for my upcoming appointment, but he had planted a seed—or maybe something more akin to an irritating burr—in my mind. I could not let the prospect go, and I didn't.

I began to sort things out on the two-hour drive up the Garden State Parkway (GSP) on the way home. Fauzia slept, and I pondered.

It was past midnight when I turned off the Garden State Parkway, putting the last of the predictably annoying tollbooths behind me and heading toward home when it hit me.

In medical school, our professor of neurology was fond of pop quizzes. He liked to catch us unprepared by posing a surprise question. It was not unlike real life, he alluded. A patient comes in with certain symptoms and you must make a diagnosis. You don't study for such an event; you must know it right away. To that end, his pop quizzes would in effect become case studies. Here are the symptoms, the patient, and the situation; now find the problem. Somewhere in there is the answer. There was a protocol under these circumstances, he would stress, a simple line of questions that would lead to an answer.

First, where is the lesion? Second, what kind of lesion is it? Third, how do you treat it?

Pulling into my driveway, I decided to give myself an early-morning pop quiz. It would be a rational and logical way to apply my own medical knowledge. As Fauzia and I entered the house through the garage after our long evening, she headed immediately upstairs to bed, and I went straight to my study, energized. It was 1:30, but I felt no desire to sleep. I needed to get to work.

I began scribbling notes of a case study on a yellow legal pad I had pulled off my desk.

A fifty-four-year-old man who had previously been the picture of good health wakes suddenly in severe pain. Quickly he realizes that though he is producing tears, they serve no useful function and his eyes are constantly dry. He is beginning to notice signs of paralysis on the left side of his face and so on and so on.

Question 1: Where is the lesion?

I remembered well the anatomy of the facial nerve from my medical school days and drew a rough sketch of that on the yellow legal pad. I needed to study it closely. One thing became clear. The problem was not in my brain. Brain lesions lead to different sets of symptoms than mine. Wherever the problem was, whatever it was, it was lower than the brain.

Once the facial nerve leaves the brain, there is still a long path, but at least I now knew I could focus on the segment of the nerve after it left the brain. But where?

After it leaves the brain, the facial nerve passes through a bony canal in the skull ultimately exiting through a small hole in the mastoid bone behind the ear. It then traverses between the two layers of the parotid gland and splits into five new branches, with each smaller branch traveling like an irrigation canal to different areas of the face.

There was still a long way to go in my analysis, but at least I could now focus on the different branches of the nerve after it emerged from my brain. My thinking became more focused. If one of these "irrigation canals" was blocked, anything below that blockage would be affected; it would be "dry" as it were.

As the early-morning hours approached dawn, I continued to systematically analyze all the various branches. It became a process of elimination.

You may recall my analogy that the upper eyelid is like a windshield wiper. The blink reflex, the up-and-down movement of the upper eyelid, spreads the tear all over the cornea, thus lubricating it.

Shortly after exiting the brain, the facial nerve sends a branch to the lacrimal gland, a gland that produces tears. I was still making plenty of tears, but because I could not blink, the tears simply rolled off and out of my eyes. It was actually a paradoxical situation, plenty of tears—but dry eye. Since I was producing tears, the problem had to be after that. I moved on. Further down, another branch reaches out to a tiny bone in the inner ear, the stapedius, which is essential for hearing.

My hearing was normal. I dug up the report of a recent hearing test I had. The audiologist had, indeed, stated that stapedius function was normal. Move down.

Another branch extended to the taste buds. I had fully normal taste, so that was not affected. Move down farther.

I had now shrunk the problem area to less than an inch, the part of the nerve that traveled through the parotid gland before splitting up into five branches. This meant I needed to focus on the area around the parotid. So now I knew where. The lesion, the cause for my facial paralysis, was definitely somewhere in and around parotid gland. This was huge. I did *not* need that surgery after all. The energy continued, and I hardly noticed that I didn't sleep that night. Fueled by Munir's encouragement and faith in me, I continued.

I continued my pop quiz.

What kind of lesion is it?

I made a list of the types of illnesses that could involve the facial nerve in very broad terms. Was there an injury or some type of trauma or a surgery? No. Was there some sort of foreign body that had found its way near there? No. Had I had an infection of some kind? Not only had I had no symptoms of any infection, such as fever, earache, sore throat, or rash, but also by that time, I had had all kinds of tests for hidden infections and they had all had come back negative. There was no infection.

Was there a *chronic* inflammation of some kind, maybe lupus or multiple sclerosis or some immune disorder? No again. I had no other symptoms and had been thoroughly tested for these. My anxiety began to increase ever so slightly, my heartbeat picking up pace. The reality was edging ever closer. That left only one answer. There was some type of growth near the parotid gland. I could put some safe money down on that, I thought.

My facial paralysis had been growing increasingly more pronounced and was getting worse. It was progressive, not static. It became clear at that point in my pop quiz that I was looking at a tumor. Though I did not want to admit it, that answer fit nicely though uncomfortably in that definition.

It was getting lighter outside by then, and I was beginning to hear the first indication of life outside my study, a car driving by, a pair of men laughing as they jogged past.

I had one last question on the early-morning quiz: What kind of tumor, then? Was it benign or malignant? A benign tumor, because of its very nature, will generally just push or skirt around another body tissue nearby. It will tend not to invade or attack it. A benign tumor usually would not disrupt the downstream activity of the facial nerve, which was clearly disrupted in my case. In stark contrast, a malignant tumor would aggressively attack the surrounding tissues and disrupt everything.

There are some benign tumors, such as neuromas, that originate from the facial nerve itself and may cause paralysis. However, those are very rare and the paralysis often waxes and wanes with periods of improvement. Mine never improved; it only worsened.

I was clearly dealing with a tumor. It was most likely in my parotid gland, and it was most likely malignant. My late-night effort had just awarded me a jarring answer I could not avoid. It was a horrible conclusion, and soon my entire family would have to face the reality of what I had just discovered.

For a student, it would be a matter of great pride being the first one to arrive at the correct answer. But as I stared at the results, I found myself wishing I had just failed the pop quiz or perhaps had missed something critical. I refused to accept my own conclusion and went over everything again, hoping I had overlooked some small detail.

But I came up with the same result, and I was suddenly horrified. There was no escape. As Fauzia and Daniyal slept comfortably and blissfully upstairs, I felt suddenly alone and far from them in my study. The early-morning stillness and quiet felt as if they were pressing in on me. It was a grim pressure, and I caught my breath.

I had cancer. It was a malignant tumor. "It just can't be," I thought grimly.

But it was.

CHAPTER 5

WELCOME TO
NEW YORK CITY

My old passport is still tucked away upstairs, having lost its usefulness long ago. But during its time, it opened doors that brought me into a new and fascinating part of my life. It bears the photo of a younger me with a wistful confidence and was taken in Karachi. But my expression belied a rather large and hidden reservoir of social naïveté that would soon be exposed in the rollicking New York City life into which I was about to immerse myself.

On one page is the fading date, stamped as I passed through customs at JFK airport, fresh off a BOAC fight from London and into a new and amusingly puzzling world: December 30, 1970.

My transition from Pakistan to America was relatively smooth, a mixture of what I had expected gently seasoned with some surprises. One of the greatest surprises was a magical snowfall my first night in New York. More subtle was the reality that despite my years of schooling, I had much to learn in the ways of the American dance known as dating. In that area, I would quickly realize, I was a babe in the woods, perhaps a kindergartener in a large and raucous school of sophisticates who had been at it much longer than I. I'd also soon discover that while American food lacked the explosive fusion of delightful spices I was used to, its dating scene did not.

Another pleasant surprise occurred three days later, after I finished my first night on call at New York Infirmary. My inability to understand the thick, slow, mumbling drawls of some of the nursing staff would serendipitously and erroneously elevate me in their eyes to high status as the exceptionally caring new doctor on call. Of course, this perception was not exactly true, as I will explain later.

The New York City I first saw in December 1970 was a far different place than the one that now bustles twenty-five miles away as I sit here writing in Ridgewood. New York City in 1970 was grittier, edgier, trying to escape the blight that had been gradually overtaking it for years.

Just a week before I stepped off the plane and onto the tarmac at JFK, construction workers had topped off the north tower of an ambitious construction project called the World Trade Center—a building that would transform Lower Manhattan—and then so many years later become an icon of tragedy. With that new thrust of construction, its height passed even the august Empire State Building, which had been the world's tallest.

The musical *Hello, Dolly!* closed at the St. James Theater on West Thirty-Fifth Street after 2,844 performances, and Paul McCartney had just filed suit to dissolve the Beatles. In

Washington, the ink was still fresh from President Richard Nixon's signing of a bill creating OSHA, a new government workers' safety agency that would have absolutely no effect on the grueling hours I was about to begin at New York Infirmary.

However, I was blissfully and excitedly unaware of all of this when I ventured out into the New York landscape.

After my brief phone conversation with my brother Javed, I signed the contract with New York Infirmary, quit my house job in Multan, packed up my bags, said my good-byes, and left for Karachi to spend my last few weeks in Pakistan with my family. Before I left Multan, I visited Professor Shaukat Raza and informed him that I had decided to head to New York. He was obviously disappointed but took it well. Perhaps deep down, he had always expected me to leave.

In Karachi, Javed filled me in on pretty much anything and everything to expect in the upcoming new phase of my life. He had been to the States and had had a taste. And it was appetizing enough to call him back. He would soon return as well, to a position in the Department of Psychiatry at the New Jersey University of Medicine and Dentistry in Newark.

I had been torn and tenuous about going. I loved what I was doing and had been looking forward to making my mark in Pakistan. But Javed's experience with the parochialism and petty jealousies of the Karachi medical community had planted the seed that I should at least take a look at what was going on elsewhere and see how I might fit in and grow. Javed also convinced me that the American system of training young doctors, the internships and residencies, was the best in the world.

Despite my initial reluctance to leave, once the decision was made, I was fully on board. There was never a second thought. I was elated and excited and eagerly looking forward to my life in America. If I had any doubts at the time, I don't remember them now. Besides, as I was preparing to leave, I was fairly certain that I would be returning to Pakistan after my residency, even though Javed's poor experience with the medical community in Karachi was always in the back of my mind.

My family, my parents in particular, had mixed emotions about my leaving. They knew this was an exciting opportunity for me, and they were happy about that. Yet, the prospect of their baby moving halfway across the world was quite distressful. It did help that they had gone through this once before with Javed, who was a trailblazer for me.

Their biggest concern seemed to be something else. Several years earlier, one of my cousins had gone to America for education, promptly fell in love with and married a girl there, and never returned home, even for visits. That, they felt, was not a path they wanted me to follow.

This ambivalence about my staying in America was to cost me a once-in-a-lifetime opportunity a couple of years later. Javed, who was heading off for a brief work stay in Scotland before he too landed back in the United States, boarded a Pakistan International Airlines flight in Karachi bound for London with me on December 29, 1970. The first of several surprises that lay in wait for me came next when I looked up in the Heathrow departure lounge to see

Javaid, a close friend from medical school. He would join me on the trip to New York.

Sitting on the runway in London, waiting for takeoff, I felt I was so well prepared for what was waiting in New York that nothing would surprise me. I was wrong, of course. My education about America had come not only from Javed but also from television. I had seen plenty of Hollywood versions of what it was like in Chicago and New York City, and I had also become quite a fan of *The Fugitive* and *The Man from UNCLE* television shows I had watched on Pakistan TV. It's funny to think about it now, having lived in the United States for so long. It must be the same for others who travel abroad, desperately searching for a recognizable program on TV to bring a sense of comfort and familiarity, only to find reruns of *Cheers* or *Taxi* in Ukrainian or Chinese.

In Karachi, Javed had tutored me about what would later prove to be an essential American survival skill: ordering from any of the ubiquitous fast-food places I found on just about every corner. His lecture included where to eat, what and how to order, and how much to pay.

"Go to McDonald's," Javed told me. "Order a burger, chips, and a Coke, and give them one dollar. You'll even get five cents back. Pocket your change and walk out, twirling your mustache"—a Punjabi phrase describing a happy and satisfied man.

"I can do that," I thought. Still, my first few days in New York had a few things that caught me unaware. The incredibly fast acceleration and deceleration of the subway trains as they sped from station to station took my breath away.

My first patient at New York Infirmary did not speak English, and I thought everyone in America spoke English.

Many strangers would ask me if I was a Puerto Rican. "What exactly is a Puerto Rican?" I wondered.

With the feminist movement in full fury in 1971, the first time I held the door open for a young woman, she chewed my head off for being a male chauvinist. But that would all change in due course. When I arrived at JFK, I was met by my friend Sarfraz, another medical school colleague who had settled in comfortably and it seemed seamlessly into New York. He greeted us with huge smiles and drove us to his apartment in Flushing, Queens, where I'd stay for two nights before heading over to my hospital apartment in Lower Manhattan. He was living then in a small apartment on the first floor of a tidy dollhouse in a quiet neighborhood of single-family homes.

On the way to his apartment, I noticed the falling flakes of what would be my first snowfall, something that never happened on the plains of Punjab. But the real snowstorm would arrive the next evening, and when the blizzard ended, there must have been something like six to ten inches of glistening white powder blanketing the neighborhood, a comfortably middle class area of compact and neat houses and friendly neighbors.

If those neighbors had looked out their front windows that night, as I'm sure they did, they would have seen three young men literally frolicking in this wondrous stuff, making snowballs, laughing, and rolling joyfully in it like little kids. I'm sure the neighbors would have lifted their curtains and wondered what was going on with these crazy young guys. It was quite the introduction to New York weather, not that I would spend a lot of time outdoors in the ensuing years. I loved it.

Sarfraz had been in New York for six months by then and had become quite popular, it seemed. He was also working as a resident in another local hospital. Despite the grueling hours, he managed to maintain an active social life. On my second night in America, he took me to a New Year's Eve party—another first and another eye-opener for me.

But first, he repeated Javed's essential tutorial for anyone fresh off the boat: how to eat in America, this time with specifics for Queens. The next afternoon, he pulled me aside.

"You must go and bring some lunch from Weston's," he said, preparing me for my first American mission.

I felt as if I were about to embark on a long and dangerous trek through a surprising and possibly lethal jungle.

"Go up the street here to 147th Street and take that up to the traffic light at Northern Boulevard. Make a right and walk a few yards until you see a large glass building with a row of circles on the roof. That's Weston's." I could feel the tension building. "Go to the counter," he continued, "and say this: 'I want three Big Ws, three medium fries, and three large Cokes.' Say that exactly."

"What is a big W?" I asked. "What is medium fries?"

"Don't worry about that. Just say it. Then give him money."

All the way down 147th Street and up Northern Boulevard, I kept repeating the mantra of the order. "Three Big Ws, three medium fries, three large Cokes." I was petrified I'd mix the order and somehow be singled out as some sort of unworthy rube. What if I said, "Three medium W's," or "Three big fries"? Would they laugh at me?

I found the Weston's and made the order. I did not mess it up. This impossible and confusing transaction went off without a hitch, and with bag in hand and change in my pocket, I returned to Sarfraz's apartment with the goods. I could not have been prouder. I had conquered my first puzzling shopping adventure.

The next step in my accelerated immersion was the New Year's Eve party. The entire concept of a New Year's Eve party was alien to me. Back then, it wasn't a common practice in Pakistan.

Sarfraz was handsome, charming, and a doctor—three universal assets that appeal to women no matter where one lives. He had settled quite seamlessly into a life in which he was certainly no stranger to the embraces of many women, with others waiting in line, apparently. Though the term is outdated these days, Sarfraz was a *playboy*, a world-class ladies' man, and he managed to juggle his women and his hectic work schedule at the hospital without missing a beat. Almost all guests at the party were young and single doctors and nurses.

Sarfraz also had a mordant sense of humor. In preparation for meeting me, he had been tutoring a number of his female admirers in what he had told them were welcoming Punjabi phrases to make me feel at home. "Say something nice to my friend Sajjad," he had told them. "He's a long way from home."

At the party, several young ladies approached me and repeated what they had been taught by Sarfraz were delightful, warm, and welcoming phrases. "Enjoy your stay," they thought they were saying. "Warm welcome and all the best in your new adventures. I hope you enjoy yourself, and we love you."

What they were actually telling me was quite another story. I can't repeat it even now, though I remember every word. Let's just say that these ladies had smilingly and innocently invited me to have relations with my mother and sister, among others. It was the filthiest language I had heard, all coming from these attractive American nurses. I was red with embarrassment, sweating. I didn't know how to react. I looked over at Sarfraz, who was enjoying himself immensely.

He had also become weary of hearing from his American friends a steady beat of how advanced things were in the United States compared with just about everywhere else in the world, including Pakistan. To counter this, he told all the nurses that Pakistani scientists had developed synthetic oranges, not juice mind you, but synthetic oranges growing on synthetic trees and synthetic watermelons too. The nurses sought me out to confirm this advancement. I did not know what to say and just nodded my head in agreement. As the party picked up its pace and the small quarters seemed to be popping with people, I soon realized two other things: I didn't know much about Western dancing, and I certainly did not know much about American food. That night, I learned about the staple comfort food known as macaroni and cheese.

This, of course, had come right on the heels of my Big W experience. I didn't know how I was going to handle it. You have to understand that Pakistani food to me is a miracle of sorts, a delightful blend of spices, each of which jumps onto the palate in a fashion that can leave one dumbfounded with pleasure. Spicy or subtle, Pakistani cooking is an art form and Pakistani food is to me a delight where cooking matched the pace of life, a slow, careful, and gentle mix.

Burgers, fries, pizza, submarine sandwiches—each was a shock, a gastronomical ambush for which I had not been prepared. Not that I did not adapt eventually. But in those early days, I was flat out shell-shocked. The assault on my taste buds started with macaroni and cheese.

At the party, I walked by a table of food and spooned several large dollops of the stuff into a huge bowl. I was hungry. After my first bite, I nearly choked at its blandness and consistency, which was not unlike a ladle full of plastic. It tasted like toothpaste and immediately sparked my interest in finding a garbage can into which I could dump it as fast as possible. I didn't know what to do with it, but I certainly had no plans of trying to eat it. I looked to Sarfraz.

"Throw it out, but be discreet about it," he said, obviously concerned I would offend the host. So I danced, offending bowl in hand, until I managed to glide by a garbage can in the corner of the kitchen. Out it went.

I faced the reality there, right in that small Queens apartment, on my first full day in America, after a Big W burger, fries, and mac and cheese, that I would have to work hard to learn to like American food. It was a huge culture shock.

The surprises continued as the clock struck midnight. Someone turned off the lights, and the next thing I knew, I was plastered by incoming kisses from Sarfraz's female friends. I was, to tell the truth, flabbergasted. I had no idea what was going on, but I knew that more than one girl had kissed me. Of course, I immediately looked to Sarfraz for guidance. But it was not about to arrive in any sort of timely fashion. He was tucked into a corner and locked in an embrace that would apparently last for the rest of the night, lips welded to one of his guests, who did not seem to mind in the least.

I was alone, but only momentarily. Enter Cookie, another adventurous and guileless friend of Sarfraz's who took a liking to me.

"Have you seen the city?" she asked.

"I've only just arrived," I said.

"It's a wonderful city," she said. "So much to see, so much excitement here, so much to do."

"I've heard," I said, missing her hints.

"Would you like a personal tour? I have a car and could drive you around. We could see the sights, certainly the Statue of Liberty and the Empire State Building. We could make a fun day out of it, really enjoy ourselves."

"Thank you very much," I told her, continuing to miss the point of her invitation. "But I'm very curious about the subway system and think I'll try to learn how to use it. I really wouldn't need your car."

"You are an idiot," Sarfraz would tell me the next morning when I mentioned Cookie's invitation. "Just as well. You're not ready for Cookie," he said.

"Welcome to New York," I thought. "I'm glad I'm not ready for Cookie."

With the preliminary introductions to New York over, I called a cab and headed into Manhattan the next day, January 1. A new year and a new experience awaited. I was on call later that night, the intern scheduled to cover medical patients scattered over all ten floors of the facility. I would get to know the entire layout quite intimately before the night was over.

The New York Infirmary, a midrise postwar building, sat on a pretty tree-lined street on East Fifteenth Street between First and Second Avenues in popular Greenwich Village. My arrangements with the hospital afforded me a free apartment across the street, free meals from the hospital cafeteria, such as they were, and free use of the hospital telephone. I would not be getting too much of a salary, but in New York, those other perks were quite comforting.

I put my two stuffed suitcases in the trunk of the cab and left Sarfraz's apartment for my new residence in Manhattan. Meeting that building's super began yet another chapter in my acclimation. A standoff of sorts started immediately. In Pakistan, he would have promptly jumped to my assistance and carried my bags upstairs, uncomplaining. In New York, the super opened the door and stared at me. He said nothing. But if I could read minds, he was saying, "I'm not going to stand here all day holding the door for you. Get in. And bring your bags with you."

I picked up on this quickly and dragged my heavy bags upstairs, where I was immediately taken by a stunning view looking north of the Empire State Building on West Thirty-Fourth Street. It was nothing short of amazing, and I quickly forgot the lack of helpfulness of the super.

What also amazed me though was how cold it was, bone-chilling in fact, both outside and inside the small studio apartment. It was only one room with a tiny alcove that was the kitchen. A thin blanket covered the mattress on a fold-out sofa bed. I started to worry about how I was going to keep from freezing later at night. But first I needed to head over to the hospital for an orientation.

Orientation helped me understand the basic geography of the hospital, which to me at the time seemed to consist of nothing but stairwells. But the orientation did nothing to help me understand the almost impenetrable accents and new expressions and local idioms that only polyglot New York could provide. It was as if everyone was speaking a new language. It was English spoken as I had never heard it before.

My tasks that first chilly night were basic and nothing new to me after my house job in Multan. We had floors of patients, and I was to be on call for the nurses who would go through the hospital switchboard to alert me of what was needed. The switchboard operator would then page me, and I would head to the nearest phone for my next assignment. For the most part, the calls were simple requests. All a nurse needed was an order for a sleeping pill for a patient or a painkiller or perhaps a laxative. It was all very routine, and for most of them, I could simply relay my response through the phone and stay in the warm comfort of my bed.

Except for one problem. I could not understand the accents of the night nurses, especially when I had just been awakened from a deep sleep. On paper, it was relatively simple, but I had no idea what they were saying. And the only way I could was to get out of the bed, get dressed, go to the hospital, find the appropriate nurse, and ask her again what she needed. My apparent attentiveness to each call, which had me running up and down the stairs all night, impressed the staff. "He is such a hardworking and caring new doctor," they thought, oblivious to my peculiar handicap.

I was off to a good start, at least in one way.

But I was also famished and burning calories to a great extent running up and down stairs all night. That first night seemed to me to be a steady and uninterrupted stream of calls. Those calls were steady enough that I did not have time to sit down or to grab a chance to eat. As the evening progressed, I could sense that the operator I had been chatting with so frequently had become an ally. After several heart-pumping hours of running the stairs, one beep after another in an uninterrupted stream of calls, I realized the hospital cafeteria was closed. The prospect of a meal was bleak.

By that time, I had also made a passing acquaintance with the operator, who over the first few hours, slowly began to show a bit of sympathy for this harried new intern who felt he had to be at the bedside of every patient. As the evening went along, she became increasingly kinder to me. "I'm sorry, another call for you," she would begin each call.

The work rules called the interns to eat when they could, to see a quick opening and grab some food, either at the cafeteria or back in their nearby apartments. There was no guarantee, of course—the patients came first—but it usually worked out. That first night, I worked three straight hours without a break, right up until 8:00 p.m. At about 8:30, the operator called to ask if I had found time to eat. "As a matter of fact, no, I haven't," I said a bit peevishly. "And I just learned the cafeteria is closed, and I have no food in my apartment."

She called back moments later. "Here is what we are going to do. Do you like fried chicken?"

"Of course," I said. But at that point, I was so famished I would have eaten anything, even macaroni and cheese.

"I'm going to order you something from Rego's Roost. When I do, I'll beep you and you go to your apartment and wait. Unless there's an emergency, I will hold your calls so you'll have a few minutes to eat."

I was touched and surprised by her kindness, and I thanked her profusely. But of course in New York where acts of kindness are often taken as a sign of weakness, she quickly brushed aside my thanks. "Don't thank me for anything. I am not paying for it; you will. Just be there to answer the door."

I can still remember that it cost me $1.98 plus a 50-cent tip. The next evening, I tracked down the operator who had so kindly arranged for my Rego's fried chicken dinner. I felt I had to thank her in person. I was touched by her small and random act of kindness.

I found her. To my surprise, she turned out to be knock-out gorgeous young woman of about thirty with blond hair and sparkling blue eyes. I nearly melted when she smiled as I entered the room housing the hospital switchboard. I thanked her, and we chatted for a while. I began thinking perhaps some magical karma was developing.

To atone for my bumbling with Cookie, I said, "I was thinking of doing some sightseeing of the city. Would you like to come along and be my guide?"

"Sure," she said with a beaming smile. "I'd love to. As long as I can bring my three kids."

I felt like an idiot and mumbled my apologies. "I am so sorry. I did not know you were married."

"Oh, that's quite OK. As we say in America, I am wed, not dead!"

Welcome to New York City.

CHAPTER 6
A RAY OF LIGHT

January 2002

In July 2001, I returned from Los Angeles after a disappointing visit to that famous clinic for facial nerve disorders. I sought phone consultations from doctors at Johns Hopkins and the Cleveland clinic, and I also called my neurologist and told him of my decision to forgo the middle fossa surgery.

"You made the right decision," he said.

At my neurologist's suggestion, I made an appointment with a highly regarded neurotologist, let's call him Dr. Roberts, at a prestigious university medical center in New York City. I had had my early-morning epiphany about a tumor in my parotid while I waited and was excited to share it with Dr. Roberts. I was optimistic I could speak to him, and together we would meet the problem head on and begin—finally—to get moving on treating my tumor and not the phantom Bell's palsy.

When I spoke with Dr. Roberts, his calm and thoughtful demeanor buoyed me. He seemed genuinely concerned and appeared to be listening. He applauded my decision to forgo surgery in California and said he understood my frustration.

Dr. Roberts was highly and unambiguously recommended. And, of course, so was that prestigious university medical center, an august institution whose reputation by almost anyone's reckoning is untainted and glowing.

It is the paradigm of how a modern hospital is supposed to work. Well funded and well run, it attracts the best of the best. Surgeons, researchers, specialists, professors, teachers, and up-and-coming medical students all covet positions there. In my mind, it certainly was the place I wanted to be treated.

Armed and in a way elated by my self-diagnosis, I went to see Dr. Roberts.

"Before we go any further," I said to the doctor as we sat across from each other in the comfort of his book-lined office, looking out on 168th Street in the Washington Heights section of northern Manhattan. His diplomas and certifications hung efficiently on the wall behind him. "Please let me present to you my own analysis and the conclusion I have reached."

I then went clearly and methodically through the steps of my early-morning analysis and explained how I had solved the puzzle of my facial paralysis. I traced the route of the facial nerve and pointed out to him how all the various branches were still intact and functioning until we arrived at the point where the nerve is embedded in the parotid.

"That is where something has gone wrong," I told him. "I think something is growing there since my paralysis is increasing. I believe it is a tumor."

I thought I had made a good, concise, and clear presentation in a very short time.

It was almost immediately after that pronouncement that it began, the first step in a subtle introduction to doctor-patient relationships in which information is important only if it lies in the hands of the doctor and flows toward the patient.

We would soon begin to bargain, though at the time, I did not know it was a one-way process. Dr. Roberts looked across his desk and pulled from his repertoire an old and well-worn cliché from a clothing store commercial that was popular at the time. "Well, well! I suppose an educated consumer is our best customer."

I wasn't sure what he meant. Was he complimenting me? For a brief moment, I had actually thought we were working together. Dr. Roberts smiled and continued, "But you have Bell's palsy, and you need decompression surgery immediately. However, instead of the middle fossa procedure, we should do the less aggressive mastoid approach."

I was stunned. Nothing I had said had registered. It was as if the good doctor had made up his mind even before seeing the patient.

Dr. Roberts continued, "Before surgery, I would like you to have an MRI of the internal auditory canal near the mastoid in back of the left ear."

Undeterred, I continued to bargain. "I can assure you there is nothing wrong in my internal auditory canal," I said. "I really would like to get an MRI of the parotid gland, because that's where the problem lies."

"Yes, of course. We can do both. Why not?" he said, though I realized later it was only to make me disappear.

Two days later, I showed up for the MRI, still confident that it would finally show there was something amiss in my parotid. I went to the reception desk and gave my name.

"So, you are here for an MRI of the internal auditory canal," she said.

"No," I said. "I'm here for an MRI of the canal *and* left parotid gland."

She showed me the order signed by Dr. Roberts for an MRI of only the auditory canal.

"I was told the MRI would include the parotid," I said. "If it does not, I will not consent to the procedure."

Surprised by my adamant reaction, she put down a folder of papers and said, "OK, let me talk to the radiologist."

"Please tell the radiologist that I am a physician," I said as I handed my business card to her.

My brief tantrum worked, and the radiologist not only agreed to scan both areas, but afterward, he showed me the scans in a gracious display of professional courtesy.

He showed me the scan of the upper part of the facial nerve.

"It looks good," he said.

"I know it's fine," I told him, "but what about the parotid?"

"Normal," he replied.

"Really?" I uttered in near shock.

That news was jolting, unsettling, like learning I had failed an exam in school.

"OK, thank you." I walked out dazed. How could that be? How could it be normal? "So much for my painstaking reasoning," I thought. "Where did I go wrong?"

By the time I was crossing the George Washington Bridge on the way home as the evening rush began to build, my confidence had returned. Things had added up so neatly and clearly in my self-diagnosis. I wasn't completely convinced there was nothing wrong with the parotid. Perhaps it was the MRI. Further research revealed that an MRI scan is not infallible and can, occasionally, fail to show a lesion. Could this be one of those infrequent occurrences?

My only hope, I realized, was to get Dr. Roberts to visually inspect my parotid gland. A few days before surgery, when I met him again to sign my consent, I threw another bargaining chip into the mix and posed an option.

"I'll consent to the decompression surgery if you, kindly, extend the incision an inch or so and make a visual check of the parotid. I'm still convinced the problem lies in there."

"That won't be a problem, I can do that," he said, though we put nothing in writing.

Later, I realized Dr. Roberts was not unlike the frazzled parent who would say anything to calm his irritating child. "Yes, tomorrow we'll go to Disney World, just go to bed now."

No problem. And thus began my surgical adventure. What sustained me as I drove to the hospital that morning for surgery was knowing that in a little more than twenty-four hours, Dr. Roberts would be sitting across from me and telling me the results of his extra exploration to my parotid. Nothing that happened in the interim would bother me, I thought, because I would finally have an answer.

The fragile house of cards I had constructed had been tenuously held together for more than nine months by my hope that I would find a solution and finally begin treatment for what I was now convinced was a malignant tumor.

When I first sat down with Dr. Roberts and agreed to a less-intrusive decompression surgery for my growing facial paralysis, I thought of him as an answer, not a problem. And though he was still convinced I had Bell's, I saw in him a glimmer of reason and understanding, and I realized I could convince him otherwise. When he agreed to take the very short side trip during surgery to look at my parotid gland, I consented to the surgery because I knew that once he did, all talk of Bell's would disappear.

Surgery of the sort I had is normally about a four-hour procedure, if you count the prep time and the time needed for closing and cleaning up. It's nothing to be trifled with, for sure, but I was not severely worried about it. I slept well the night before, and in the early-morning hours of August 5, 2001, my family drove me to the hospital.

I was certainly not nervous; that is just not in my nature. I try always to look at things in a positive light, and that predilection has never served me wrong, even in the dark hours later in my struggle. I should have been. The morning of the surgery after going through preop, I undressed, stepped into my gown, and waited to be taken into the operation theater.

A nurse entered. "Ready to go?" she asked.

"Yes, I'm ready," I said, waiting for the gurney that usually brings patients into the operating room.

"Good. An orderly will take you in."

"No gurney?" I asked. "No wheelchair?"

"No need. It's just over there," she said, pointing down the hallway.

My escort entered and took my elbow. I thought at first it was to gently lead me to the operating room. But instead he merely lifted it and placed my charts under my arm. He chattered disconcertedly as we made the uneasy walk three to four hundred feet down the hall. I had an IV pole dripping fluid into one arm with the charts tucked under the other, all while wearing that hospital gown, which did nothing to protect my modesty. It was an inauspicious start.

After the surgery, I woke up in the large recovery room, aware first of the incessant noise of nauseous surgery patients and a gaggle of nurses who wandered about the large room, attending to them. I felt woozy and needed to use the bathroom. I asked for a bedpan, but a passing nurse simply pointed to the bathroom door about thirty feet away. Still plugged into my IVs and unsteady postsurgery, I made my way there gingerly. No one gave me a second glance.

I was later moved to a semiprivate room in a wheelchair pushed by a harried orderly who paid little attention to my nausea or me. He practically ran with the wheelchair and took each of what seemed like many hallway corners at great speed. The trip was not conducive to keeping what little I had in my stomach down. I quickly realized I was about to throw up and began flailing my arms to get him to slow down. My effort had no effect, and I vomited on the floor shortly after he finally noticed and stopped.

It did not take more than a minute in my new room to be slapped by the harshness of the fetid and nearly indescribable odor that awaited me, one I was familiar with from my days as an intern. My new roommate had a gangrenous foot. While the gangrene itself might not be contagious, the bacteria that were producing the fetid odor could have spread to my freshly opened surgical wounds. Besides, the overpowering smell was doing a number on my queasy stomach.

I pointed this out to the nurse and was quickly moved to another room. As I settled uneasily in for the long night after a groggy visit with my family, I once again had the urge to use the bathroom. I pressed the call button to summon the nurse. No response. Again and again, for the next twenty minutes, I pushed the call button, to no avail. I could see a group of nurses sitting and chatting at their station, completely oblivious to my calls for help. Finally, I tried to walk to the bathroom, easing off the bed but crashing loudly to the floor, sending the IV pole and its contents flying. I vomited a bright-red mélange from the only thing I had eaten in hours, a cup of cherry Jell-O. Thinking it was blood, the nurses finally rushed in. The rest of the night was sleepless, a continuous stream of interruptions for eye drops and blood pressure and pulse checks. In the early morning, groups of interns and various residents stopped by every twenty minutes to ask the same questions.

It had been a long night, and I was tired and futilely hoping for even a catnap. I knew that was unlikely. No matter, on the grand scale of things, such irritations are trivial. I began counting the time until I would see Dr. Roberts.

I took solace from the knowledge that I had finally had my decompression surgery, and first thing in the morning, Dr. Roberts would be telling me the results of his visual inspection of the parotid gland. Wild rides around the hallways, a gangrenous roommate, and a bad night without sleep or much to eat were a fair price to pay for an end to those long months of uncertainty.

By 8:00 a.m. the next morning, after thirty hours without sleep and a failed attempt to get a breakfast, I was ready to leave.

A little after 9:00 a.m., Dr. Roberts entered my room, all smiles. "Everything went well," he said. "I did the decompression and cleaned everything out very efficiently. You are on your way to recovery."

"But what about my parotid?" I asked. "What did you see when you checked that?"

"Dr. Iqbal, that would have extended the surgery another hour. There was no need to do that. No reason at all, in fact."

Shocked and speechless, I said nothing. I was crushed. The exploratory visit of my parotid had been the main reason I had agreed to the surgery in the first place. The trust I felt I had for Dr. Roberts, the bridge on which I thought we had walked together, collapsed in that instant.

"I think you will have a very good recovery," he said, dismissing everything else. "See you in a month. Please make an appointment with my office."

Dr. Roberts left, and I called Fauzia immediately. "I want to leave right now," I told her. I was livid. I did not want to stay there a minute longer. The stabilizing hope that had held it all together was dangerously close to running dry. I had reached my tipping point, and when I stormed out, disappointed from that prestigious hospital that morning, I was beyond angry and frustrated.

My day in the hospital and the patronizing surgeon challenged my inclination toward equanimity. I had always accepted that things sometimes do not go the way I would prefer, but I was worn down. It was only a temporary sojourn into negativity, but believe me, it seemed interminable.

After I arrived home from the hospital, my anger began to dissipate. I gathered what little was left of my reserves and refocused my attention on proving my intuitions about a tumor. In hindsight, the result of that unsettling hospital experience was oddly sustaining and calming. It reaffirmed my belief that setbacks are merely short detours on the way to a goal. A few months later, I would be graced with a sweet and almost comforting dose of hope. And when hope arrives in the form of a cancer diagnosis, one must take pause to understand the depth of my frustration.

When I got home, I could not rest. I began once again to assess the situation. Why had the MRI of my parotid been negative? Was there something wrong with the MRI technique? Was there a way to improve upon it?

More research revealed one possibility. A regular MRI can at times miss something if its cross-sectional views are too wide. Imagine a loaf of rye bread with caraway seeds—the caraways standing in for a small tumor. It would be possible to slice the loaf in such a way, say one-inch slices—that no caraways would show up. But if you took thinner cross sections of the loaf, say half- or quarter-inch slices, the seeds would be visible.

I needed a more advanced MRI technique that offered those thinner slices, and I knew where I could find one, the local hospital in Ridgewood where I had sent patients and worked for thirty years. I called a radiologist I knew there.

"I am convinced that I have a tumor in my parotid gland, but an MRI was reported as negative," I told him. "I think an MRI with one- to two-millimeter slices using 3-D imaging might uncover the tumor. Can you do that for me?"

Now this was a colleague I had known for years, and I thought the request was simple. "No, I can't."

"Why on earth not?" I pleaded.

"Because you might be a doctor, but now you are a patient. Patients cannot dictate how a procedure should be done. You know nothing about MRI technique. This is my field, not yours. Sorry, can't do it."

I could not argue.

I went back to see Dr. Roberts a month later for my follow-up.

"Ah, your face looks so much better," he told me. "The operation was a success."

"No, it was not," I told him. "My face hasn't changed a bit."

I went on to explain to the increasingly incredulous Dr. Roberts that since long before the surgery, I had been taking weekly digital pictures at exactly the same angle and profile of my face. "If you would like, I can lay them out and show you. There is not one single iota of difference."

Such an effrontery, it seemed, always brought out the limpid wit of the good doctor.

"Wow," he said, a weak smile forming, "you are really up on it. We could devise a new scale for grading the facial-nerve paralysis, the Iqbal-Roberts scale—and with digital images to boot."

That short, offhand quip signaled the end of my struggle to find synergy with Dr. Roberts. I left his office and never returned.

But I was back to square one, with growing facial paralysis, no answers, and the fear of a tumor growing unchecked.

The constant dryness and discomfort in my left eye, despite all the remedies I tried, had become another source of frustration. So in early November 2001, I flew to Los Angeles to meet Dr. Levine, who implanted an ingeniously devised metal spring in my left upper eyelid, which largely restored my blink reflex. That relieved my eye symptoms, but I remained deeply concerned about the proper diagnosis of my illness.

I was not down for long. Another friend and former medical school classmate, Rasheed, who was now working in Brooklyn, heard about my problems and called to tell me about Dr. Mark May, who ran the Facial Nerve Center at the University of Pittsburgh Medical Center. In fact, my friend told me, Dr. May had written the only authentic textbook on the facial nerve.

I called the University of Pittsburgh Medical Center immediately, only to learn that Dr. May had retired, and since his retirement, the Facial Nerve Center dissolved. "Here we go again," I thought, wondering if my consistent bad luck would change at some point. It would have to.

I called Rasheed back and told him the latest development. "I will track him down for you," he promised. And he did just that, finding Dr. May in Israel where he had settled after his retirement. Dr. May suggested I call Dr. Barry Schaitkin, his protégé and coauthor of the aforementioned textbook, who was still at the medical center.

Persistence, I had learned long ago, will eventually pay off. I called Dr. Schaitkin, a genial and affable man, who explained that while the formal facial nerve center had indeed closed, everyone involved with it was still at the medical center. The closure of the center was a mere formality, he told me; the well-honed expertise was still there.

Dr. Schaitkin had no obligation to listen to my well-polished but very long story. But he did. He did not have to offer an opinion over the telephone, but he did that as well.

I gave a synopsis of my long struggle with facial paralysis and the frustrating arguments with various experts. Then, taking a deep breath, I had just started to present my own analysis when he stopped me in midsentence.

"Dr. Iqbal," he told me. "I'm afraid you must have a parotid tumor."

"Hallelujah!" I thought, breathing a big sigh of relief.

CHAPTER 7
SETTLING IN

Adjusting to life in New York City was as close to effortless as I could have hoped. My first case of nerves over ordering a burger and fries disappeared as quickly as the meal itself. I really had no choice anyway. I had committed myself, I knew where I wanted to go, and I knew if I applied myself, there would be few problems.

I leaped into New York enthusiastically with both feet, knowing full well there would be a few snags and unintended excursions along the way. Was I worried? Not at all. I was prepared, and I was excited and hungry to take a bite from all that New York had to offer. Soon after I arrived at New York Infirmary, I learned I was comfortable with the medical side of things because I had worked hard and learned well in Pakistan. Medical knowledge is the same no matter where you are.

By the end of that breathless period, I would earn the trust and admiration of several of my mentors, own a pediatric practice in New Jersey, meet and marry the sustaining love of my life, and begin a new and delightful passage. I did not know it at the time, but reinforced by these powerful, positive events, I gained a deep reservoir of hope that I would later need to dip into. We all have these reserves and they possess great potential to serve us well if we know they are there for the taking. This would provide me the strength to meet my biggest challenge with the gloves off. I would be ready to fight the cancer that had so rudely disrupted my perfect life.

During those formative years, I had the benefit of guidance from a number of mentors whose leadership, advice, and example would provide the strength I needed in so many moments of doubt.

When I started this American life class, I didn't know I would be honored, challenged, bemused, and excited. I didn't know that I would also face two crushing, almost paralyzing losses that affect me even today.

The New York City I stepped into in 1970 was starkly different from the brighter and cleaner one that people can so breezily walk around today. There was a gauzy film of desperation in some parts of the city, where people in some neighborhoods made their livings any way they could— drugs, prostitution, gambling, petty crimes. Gentrified and upscale neighborhoods, like Park Slope, the Bowery, or even most of Forty-Second Street, known as Times Square, where today families stroll breezily through squeaky-clean stores and bright lights, were, in those days, ugly and grimy and not sections of New York you would expose your family to unnecessarily. Crime was everywhere, even on the trains of New York, where passengers were often robbed, assaulted, and even shot.

For the most part, my daily existence revolved around work and learning. My hospital rounds were my first and sometimes my only priorities. Mind you, I'm not saying I was a hermit. I was young, full of energy, and tirelessly curious. Even though I was working like a dog, I still managed to go out at times—maybe to see a play or an occasional movie with friends. However, my life was not like the lives of my nonmedical friends, who would dive smoothly into Friday-to-Sunday parties and all that went with them. But it did have a few perks.

When I arrived at New York Infirmary, I was given the option of a straight pediatric internship or the rotating type that allowed one to experience several specialties of medicine. I was inclined to pediatrics, loved it in fact. But in the back of my mind was just a gnat of a question, a slight nagging. What if I found something else that appealed to me more? In my house job in Multan, I had done nearly a year in pediatrics and had come to love it, but I didn't know much about the appeal of other disciplines.

I opted for the rotation, but once you fall in love, it's difficult to spend time with someone or something else. So while I was doing surgery and internal medicine, thoughts of pediatric medicine were never far from my mind.

That was confirmed one day when I was examining a newborn under the supervision of an attending physician, Abbas Taheri. He watched from a distance and then complimented me on my handling and care of the young child. "Have you ever thought of becoming a pediatrician?" he asked.

Indeed I had, and that was all I needed to hear. "Pediatrics has always been my first love," I told him, "and now I feel I've been wasting an entire year doing these rotations."

Dr. Taheri stopped in his tracks as we walked down a quiet hallway to the next patient's room. He raised a wagging finger at me, suspended in the fluorescent lights.

"Don't ever say that again," he admonished me. "Honest work and an honest experience will never be a waste of time, and one day, you will find this most useful."

It was a prescient and prophetic statement that I remembered later when I moonlighted as an emergency-room physician and beyond when I began my fight with cancer. No experience is ever wasted if one can learn from it. Even today, in my practice, I have no problem with suturing a cut, removing a wart, or doing many other tasks not normally done by a pediatrician, all because of the things I learned during my rotation.

Forty years later, I understand what he meant. I never said anything about the rotation schedule again. Dr. Taheri was not the only mentor to impart wisdom I still carry with me. Another was Mortimer Webber, an erudite and uncommonly thoughtful and gentle man, who was the chairman of the department of pediatrics at New York Infirmary. Above all other awards and accolades, he was kind, and he would become a second father to me, perhaps something I, as a young man thousands of miles from home, needed desperately, I suppose, because I was so far from my own father and his gentle, loving influence. A few years later, Dr. Webber would play a dramatic and major part in my life when he reneged on a promise upon which I had mistakenly counted.

During my time at New York Infirmary, I also made a wonderful connection with another attending physician who would make his rounds with me. Robert Schacht, a pediatric nephrologist, stepped in to help during one of the most painful events of my young life, offering his assistance and knowledge to the physicians attending to my seriously ill sister, who was suffering from kidney failure in Karachi. Making rounds together for three months, we established a strong rapport as he listened to my questions and watched me interact with patients. Dr. Schacht was apparently impressed enough with me to later offer me a fellowship with him at the prestigious New York University Medical Center. A fellowship is the last and most-sought-after rung on the ladder of a young doctor's training.

I wish only that the circumstances that allowed him to get to know me were slightly different—that my sister's fatal illness was not part of our discussions.

I left New York Infirmary in June 1973 with a bang and a send-off I did not expect. I'd come a long way during the two and a half years since I had stepped off the plane and into a brave new world.

At the intimate ceremony of newly crowned graduates and an appreciative faculty, fanning himself occasionally with the certificates he was handing out, Dr. Webber broke the steady rhythm of the doctors walking to the stage. As I strolled up to him to get my certificate, he stopped and grabbed my hand.

"Hold on a minute," he told the audience, stopping the dance and locking his eyes on mine. I noticed he was on the verge of tears and began to feel a few of my own slowly forming. "I have to tell you something about this young man," Dr. Webber said, looking out at the audience. "Every year, we have a new batch of residents. All are good, or they would not be here. Of those, I always find one or two each year I would rate as exceptional. And then once in a great while, if you are lucky enough, you come across someone like Dr. Iqbal."

For the next few minutes, he went on to say how much he had enjoyed teaching me and how he would miss me. "I hope he has learned well during his stay here. I know I have learned a thing or two from him." I couldn't believe it. This was high praise indeed and completely unexpected. As I walked back to my seat, stunned—exuberant at such a wonderful comment, yet deeply humbled and overwhelmed by it—I passed another of my supervisors who stopped me for a pat on the back.

"Another Dr. Spock, I see," she said.

I had managed during those hectic days, in what little spare time I had, to become a fan of the television show *Star Trek*, as were many other young people in those days. "Dr. Spock," I thought. "Are my ears that big?"

I did not make the connection with Dr. Benjamin Spock, the world's best-known pediatrician, whose book *Baby and Child Care* had launched the parenting careers of so many millions.

Dr. Webber was to show his faith in me in a more concrete way, allowing me in effect to graduate in June when I actually had six more months to go. Because I had begun my stint at New York Infirmary in January 1971, I was off schedule and would have missed the chance to apply for the residency programs in other, more prestigious hospitals because those always opened in July. With his blessing and a strong recommendation, I was heading to a senior residency program at St. Luke's Hospital, a premier institution in Harlem, in July 1973. I was on a roll.

As good as my training was at New York Infirmary, the residency at St. Luke's was far more comprehensive and rigorous. I would learn more during one year of pediatric training at Saint Luke's than I did during the entire thirty months at New York Infirmary. It was a heady time, invigorating, and immensely enjoyable. I saved a young boy's life, in fact, in a way that was dramatic enough to make the pages of the *New York Post*.

I was on call as the senior pediatric resident on a frigid Saturday afternoon in January when I was paged to the emergency room. Police had brought in a five-year-old boy, unconscious and barely clinging to life. He and a friend had been playing on a Central Park lake that had not completely frozen over. The ice was tempting but not safe. He had fallen through, been completely immersed in the frigid water for fifteen to twenty minutes, and had drowned, literally. His life was hanging by a fragile thread of hope provided by the brave and conscientious police officers who pulled him out of the frigid lake and continued resuscitation efforts until their arrival at the emergency room. Technically, the young boy was dead.

As I took charge of the resuscitation efforts, I was plagued by a nagging doubt that too much time had passed, that our work was futile. But we continued, because we also hoped that in the time the boy was submerged in the frigid water, hypothermia had set in and protected his brain.

I inserted a tube through his throat into the trachea so we could attach a breathing device, called an Ambu bag, a manually operated resuscitation device that was more efficient than mouth-to-mouth. Like a well-oiled machine, the entire team of health professionals worked in total harmony. Someone did heart compressions, and another started an IV and administered drugs as needed. Another drew blood samples to frequently monitor the oxygen levels. Yet another kept a meticulous minute-by-minute record of everything we did. It was a controlled and efficient frenzy. And it worked. After nearly an hour, the young man began to breathe on his own, even though not efficiently.

He was still very unstable and in critical condition, but it was nothing short of a miracle that he had survived. We put him on a ventilator and admitted him to the pediatric intensive care unit. I decided it was critical that I continue to supervise his care and personally monitor this miracle boy. So I stayed by his bedside the rest of the weekend, monitoring his clinical status and the lab results, changing his medications as he improved, adjusting the ventilator settings and managing the intravenous fluid therapy. I hardly slept. Through it all, I frequently sought guidance from my attending pediatrician, Dr. Allendorf, and was most ably assisted by the junior resident, Dr. Rivera.

By Monday morning, he had regained consciousness and was completely out of danger. My chief rewarded my efforts on Monday with an exceedingly rare permission to "go home and get some sleep"—the Holy Grail every resident dreams of and covets.

Throughout the weekend, the boy's distraught mother was right there, frightened, exhausted, tense, and cautiously hopeful I was doing the right things to keep her son from dying. As things progressed and pointed to recovery, she slowly relaxed and we seemed to develop a tight bond. Tuesday, after a wonderful and rare full night of sleep, I stopped into the ICU to say hello to the boy and his mother.

"Mira, mira!" she said excitedly. "Look! Here is Dr. Iqbal, who saved your life. Say hi to him."

In a movie, this would be the moment the boy would look with grateful, tearful eyes at the wonderful young doctor who had given him a new chance at life and jump into my arms for an appreciative embrace. A crescendo of inspiring music would fill the movie theater, and the audience would move to the edges of their seats. Instead, he seemed to recoil at the attention. He gave me a look that said quite clearly, "Who the hell is this guy?" He remembered nothing.

Tuesday's *Post* had it all on page 5, including my name. That was perhaps the nicest thing of all—that some colleague took the time to talk to a reporter and give me the credit. I never did learn who that was, but I remain appreciative.

And while I was at St. Luke's, I had the unusual and most comforting knowledge that I had climbed the next rung on the ladder.

Robert Schacht, whom I had gotten to know so well, had offered me a fellowship at NYU Medical Center after I finished my residency at St. Luke's. It was unique and rewarding to know I had a fellowship waiting for me. What a relief to know I might not have to join the mad, sometimes-desperate search that always ensued toward the end of residency training, a time of uncertainty to add to the already large number of sleepless nights.

This brought me great peace of mind, as did another encouraging note from the chairman of our department at St. Luke's as I left that program a year later. "To Dr. Iqbal," Doris Whethers inscribed on the flyleaf of a book she gave me as a parting gift, "The Star of St. Luke's."

Another act of kindness. Another gift of confidence I would need later. But there were other times when the light was not as bright. While I was still at New York Infirmary in late December 1972, I learned that my beloved sister, Zahida, the bright star in our family of boys, the girl whose wedding and departure had left me grief-stricken as a young boy, was in perilous condition in a Karachi maternity home. She had suffered complications during a Caesarian delivery that led to complete kidney failure and the resultant coma. I had consulted with Robert Schacht about what could possibly be done, and he even went so far as to speak to her doctors.

On December 30, 1972, I spoke with my family in Karachi and was buoyed by the news that Zahida appeared to be doing better. Her eyes had been fluttering, I learned, and she had even opened them momentarily. I thought at the time how nice it would be to put my fears about Zahida behind me and to begin a new journey with a bit of brightness.

But on New Year's Eve, she died.

The grim news from Pakistan came in the form of a brief phone call that left me brokenhearted and stricken with unbearable grief. Crushed and literally reeling, I knew I needed to find my brother Javed, who was then living in the Greenwich Village neighborhood of New York City. I had to see him. The thought of relaying the dark news over a telephone, of actually saying aloud that Zahida had died, was too much to contemplate. I felt for the first time too far away from the sweet comfort and succor of my family, and I knew I had to lean on Javed. He was my only link to home, my older and wiser brother who had helped me so much.

As were many countless others in New York City that New Year's Eve, Javed and his fiancée, Wanda, had plans to bring in 1973 in style, with a celebration. I needed to hurry and catch them before they left home. I found my car and began the fifteen-minute drive downtown. God knows how I made it, sobbing and crying the entire way. I didn't care or even notice the passersby who must have looked at me as a madman behind the wheel. I was vaguely aware of the traffic lights and cars around me. It was a miracle I even made it, but I did, and I found parking right near his apartment.

As I turned the corner to Javed's front door, walking, reeling like a drunk on that crazed evening, I saw Javed and Wanda just emerging from the door, dressed for an evening on the town. Our eyes met. I said nothing. There was no need. He gently dropped Wanda's hand and stared briefly at me. Then we ran into the comforting embrace of each other's arms, tears flowing down our cheeks. Wanda came over and wrapped her arms around both of us. Sharing our grief, she understood that we needed to be alone.

That night in my apartment, as the city celebrated a New Year and the loud and jubilant crowds roared and screamed, "Happy New Year!" just outside my window, we two brothers sat alone in chairs, facing each other, consumed by immense grief. A small table lamp provided the only light in the darkened room. Nothing was said. Occasionally one of us would reach out for a brief hug or place a hand on a knee or squeeze a shoulder, engulfed in our own private sorrows. But together, the weight of it was more tolerable. There was so much joy in the world outside, yet so much sadness inside our hearts.

It was the saddest day of my life.

Almost a year later, my immense sorrow was buried and resting where it still lies. Robert Schacht provided me with another wonderful moment and showed me how graciousness can extend to even the most pedestrian job search. By then, well into my residency at St. Luke's, he called to check in on me and to assess my interest in the pediatric nephrology fellowship he had offered earlier.

"I want you to think again that this will be primarily a research fellowship with less emphasis on the clinical side of things. You should consider this, and you should see what else is out there before you agree to take it."

I said I realized that but was still interested.

"You need to explore other fellowship offers," he told me again. "See what's out there. You may like some other opportunity better. My offer will be waiting for you if nothing else interests you. But you should know what's out there."

So I applied for a fellowship position in pediatric nephrology in New York Cornell Medical Center, a program headed by Dr. John Lowry. I sometimes look back on my discussion with Dr. Lowry and wonder how different things could have been. But I also realize now that that interview focused a light on something I had been avoiding with great and clear intention—family pressure to get married.

After an engaging and positive discussion with Dr. Lowry, he stopped and asked me a question, intimating that he would hire me based on my response. I suppose it was a question on the minds of many of my mentors at the time. "Are you going back to Pakistan?" By that time, I was increasingly thinking more of staying than going back, but I had not ruled anything out or in.

"I like it here," I told Dr. Lowry, "and would like to stay here." I suppose that was what he wanted to hear. "But," I added, "a lot would depend on who I marry and what she wants to do. I would like a decision on something like that to be one we would make together. If I marry a Pakistani girl and she wants to go back to Pakistan, then so be it."

Dr. Lowry, sitting across the table from me, raised his hand and pushed back his chair. "Wow. That changes everything. The thing is, Dr. Iqbal, I was hoping that we would have a long association where, in time, you would assume more and more of my responsibilities. I'm not looking to train you for two years only to have you leave after that."

That was the end of that. I often wonder how different things might have been if I had given a slightly different answer. Ironically, I did marry a Pakistani girl, but she had no desire to go back. As my father had taught me so many times, it always pays to be honest. I have no regrets about my answer that day.

I would later spend two wonderful years under Dr. Schacht as a pediatric nephrology fellow. But in the meantime, I had to finish up at St. Luke's and face the music about marriage. My own defiance about being told whom I should marry and a large dose of luck both worked in my favor. Mind you, I was not in a rush to marry, but as happens in all families, pressure from my parents at home intervened. My mother and father were nervous, worried that I would marry an American girl and never return home.

In December 1973, I went back to Pakistan for a visit and learned that my parents had lined up a number of young women they wanted me to meet. Their goal was to convince me to agree to an arranged marriage, as was our Pakistani custom back then. I wanted absolutely no part of that, and though I like to think of myself as a dutiful son, I refused to meet anyone, despite my parents' best efforts.

It was then that my sister-in-law Bano Baji entered the game. Bano, who was married to my brother Mansoor, seemed to be quite fond of the daughter of a friend, a young woman named Nuzzo. For days, our conversations varied little.

"You must meet Nuzzo."

"No."

"I think it's time you have a chat with Nuzzo."

"No."

To me, it was like Chinese water torture, and it reached the point and became so annoying that I finally slammed my open hand down on a table and actually yelled, "Nuzzo, Nuzzo, Nuzzo! I don't ever want to hear that name again."

Then I stormed out of the room, Bano staring at me openmouthed. How little did I know what the future would hold for me.

But my parents took this responsibility to marry me off to a proper bride seriously, to the point that my father, suspecting that I had someone tucked away back in New York, took to his bed and would not get up. He was sure when I left I would not be returning. That is known in many circles as intense parental pressure, and I succumbed. The day I left, I promised my father I would be back in three months, not, of course, having the slightest idea how I would pull off that magic, considering I had no vacation time left at St. Luke's. It occurred to me on the flight back that all senior residents were allowed a one-month paid elective of their own choosing to further hone their skills in whatever discipline they were interested in. Most elected to go to some top-notch hospital in New York to further their knowledge of pediatric cardiology, neurology, neonatology, or other related fields.

For my one-month elective, I decided it would be in tropical medicine. And where better to study tropical medicine than in the tropics, say, at a hospital in Karachi, Pakistan.

It was hard to argue with that pretzel logic, and luckily for me, no one did. Dr. Whethers, surprised as she was, approved my odd request, and in April, I was back in Pakistan, ready for my tropical medicine training and for a steady stream of potential wives. The time had come. I decided to face it head-on and dive in.

For two weeks, I met several young women, none of whom swayed my inclination to remain single. To be fair, it could very well be true that they felt the same about me, but I don't know.

As the time for my departure approached, panic set in. My family was getting desperate, except for my sister-in-law Bano, who had remained completely aloof and silent. She had not forgotten or forgiven my tantrum four months back. Finally, she approached me.

"You were very disrespectful to me, my dear little brother, when you told me not to mention Nuzzo again. And I swore to myself I would not. But as I watch this going on, I feel sorry for you. So I will tell you one more time, Nuzzo is the only right one for you. Do you want to meet her?"

"Yes, please," I said meekly.

So Bano called Nuzzo over to their house on some sort of pretext, and I met her briefly for the first time. Now Bano was a university-educated career woman, but it's important to understand that this did nothing to undermine her conservative bent. She thought the few minutes I had spent with Nuzzo would be enough to convince me I should marry her.

"I'd like to get to know her a bit," I protested.

"You cannot date. This is Pakistan after all."

"Too bad then," I replied, ever the rebel.

Then fate—perhaps—intervened. The next day, Bano became sick, and as the convenient family doctor, I tended to her while she lay in bed at home. I'm still not certain if this was a well-planned setup, but also tending to her, so conveniently, was the daughter of her good friend Nuzzo.

It was a perfect and seamless way for two young people to get to know each other. We talked for days about everything—life, love, philosophy, and dreams—free of the usual dating detritus and nosy chaperones. We had three days of wonderful conversation without the pressure of dating or arrangements or anything else.

It was nothing short of wonderful and all provided by the providential sickness of Bano. At the end of it, Bano, recovered, asked what I thought.

"She's absolutely wonderful."

As was customary, Bano went to Nuzzo's father for his permission for our marriage.

His wife had died several years ago, and he had devoted his life to raising his three daughters as a single parent.

He was a wonderful and open-minded man, and he responded just as expected. "I would never force her to do anything against her wishes," he said. "I need to know how she feels about it."

"Don't worry. I have already asked her."

"And?"

"She said yes."

We had nine frenzied days to prepare for the wedding before I had to head back to New York. That meant meeting the requisite relatives, having them gauge my appropriateness, having my wedding clothes made, sending out invitations, arranging for entertainment and tons of food— and then of course the wedding itself. It was no small feat, considering that Pakistani weddings are traditionally lavish three-day affairs. A challenge, for sure, but we pulled it off. My Nuzzo shined like the bright diamond I knew she was. Everything was impeccable.

The tailors charged with making my wedding suit, knowing I was from New York, chose heavy wool, thinking of winters that were never seen in Karachi. They did a wonderful job, considering the timing, but wool was not particularly suitable for an April wedding in the Karachi heat.

I skipped the suit and was married on April 22, 1974, in the best of 1970s fashions, a wide-lapelled pastel jacket complete with a flowery pattern and white polyester double-knit pants. I looked as if I were heading for the Strip in Las Vegas.

One of the last things we did in the chaos of the wedding preparations was designing, printing, and mailing out invitations. As I slipped the first one into an envelope to be mailed, I was startled to find that I was not marrying Nuzzo, but someone named Fauzia.

I was greatly relieved to know that Nuzzo was Fauzia's nickname. We, of course, are still married today more than forty years later. I was lucky to have found my soul mate so early in life.

Two days later, I was on my way back to America. Fauzia/ Nuzzo joined me four months later after obtaining her visa.

Our beautiful union must have provided an impetus for Javed and Wanda, because shortly after that, they decided to tie the knot as well. Acutely sensitive to my parents' misgivings about an American daughter-in-law, they wisely went to Pakistan so Wanda could meet my parents and gain their blessings. They arrived in Karachi in November 1974. I am sure there were plenty of trepidations on both sides, but the moment Wanda stepped off the Pakistan International Airlines' jumbo jet dressed in Pakistani clothes and my parents got the first glimpse of her, they promptly fell in love with her. Wanda reminded them of Zahida, whose loss, it seemed, was insurmountable.

Wanda had lost her father shortly before that trip, and she and my father bonded instantly. It was as if Wanda had found her father again and my father had been reunited with his daughter. My parents not only gave their blessings but also made all the arrangements for the marriage ceremony to take place in Karachi two weeks later.

Javed and Wanda stayed in Pakistan for about a month. Those were among the happiest days of my father's life. Every morning, Wanda would tiptoe into his bedroom, wake him up, and lovingly comb his hair, and then she would sit there, chatting with him for what seemed like hours. There were sightseeing trips, picnics to Hawke's Bay on the seashore, and day tours on private boats. I still have a picture of the two of them riding a camel in an amusement park on Clifton Beach in Karachi. There was a never-ending glow of happiness on my father's face. It was nothing short of wonderful; the fates had found alignment. All was right in the world again—or at least in Karachi.

As Javed and Wanda were leaving Pakistan, they sat down with my parents and made plans for a reunion in New York in the spring of 1975. It never took place. In January 1975, my father passed away, suddenly and unexpectedly, from complications of a fairly routine prostate surgery.

Undoubtedly, my father was the most important figure in my life. More than anyone else, he shaped my personality, not by lectures but by how he lived, the way he took care of his family, the manner in which he treated others, the calmness with which he faced crises and hardships, and all the unspoken words through which he conveyed to me with absolute clarity how he expected me to live my life. Those are still my guiding principles.

By the time I finished my NYU fellowship under Dr. Schacht, I knew I wanted my own practice in pediatrics with a subspecialty in nephrology. I was finally done with school and ready for life. My mentor, Dr. Webber, with whom I had been in constant contact since leaving New York Infirmary, had a practice in Midtown Manhattan near Gramercy Park. He asked me to join him in his practice as his associate and, eventually, take it over when he retired in the very near future.

By then, Javed was living in Bergen County, New Jersey, and had become chief of psychiatry at Bergen Pines Hospital in Paramus, which led me to learn of a family practice for sale in nearby Ridgewood. I heard its owner was about to retire and was interested more in finding a compassionate doctor to whom he would hand over his patients than making a killing on the sale.

Though I still assumed I'd soon be taking over Dr. Webber's Manhattan practice, primarily on Javed's insistence, I thought I should at least meet the New Jersey doctor.

Given my decision on pediatrics, I did not really want a family practice.

The doctor somehow found something in me that met his needs. And he insisted I was the one. "Take over my practice, take over the existing patients, and then gradually become a pediatrician," he said. "I'll know my patients are in good hands, and you can gradually establish your own pediatric practice," he insisted. He had already been offered $25,000, he told me, but he would give me his entire practice for free.

He said he would also leave me all his furniture, instruments, and remaining supplies and rent his building to me below market value. My side of this enticing bargain was to take care of his patients and gradually transition to pediatrics. I was still inclined to take over Dr. Webber's practice in Gramercy Park and mentioned to him only briefly the New Jersey offer.

"Sajjad," Dr. Webber told me once he quickly gauged my new opportunity, "take a look around here," indicating Gramercy Park, which, like much of Manhattan at the time, was worn and tired and headed downhill.

"Ridgewood and Bergen County is where a young man should be," he said. "It's where you should go and raise a family. New York City and Gramercy Park is not the place for that or for you. My practice here is dying."

"But, Dr. Webber," I protested, "for months, I have planned on accepting your offer. This New Jersey idea was not part of the equation. I have chosen to take your offer."

"My son," he said, "the offer has just been rescinded."

CHAPTER 8

THE GLOVES COME OFF

February 2002

B arry Schaitkin's cancer confirmation closed one door and opened another. Finally and blessedly, the wait was over.

I was elated and ready for the fight. My reaction might not have been typical, but it was genuine. I could now move ahead and get things fixed.

My longtime office manager, Pat, had a reaction that was more typical. She began to cry immediately after I told her. There would be more tears as I introduced my loved ones to the facts, but none from me.

"Don't," I would say. "Now that we know what it is, we can treat it. The real bad news was not knowing."

Any cancer diagnosis is frightening, but there are degrees of fear. Many are accompanied by an explanation of possible treatments, comforting statistics of survival rates, and reassurances from doctors of their successes. Some others come with an apology and an estimate of one's life expectancy, with less-reassuring discussions about things like quality of life and making the best of what time remains. Mortality is laid out in clipped statistics, as if life itself is defined by actuarial tables, free of the intangibles, such as will and inner strength and positive thinking. For all my years of experience, it was momentarily daunting to be on the receiving end of such a statistical analysis versus a human explanation, which was how I always tried to communicate with my patients.

In the relative world of cancer, mine was considered more "treatable." For lack of a better term, it was a "gentler" cancer. But that's like saying it was a mild hurricane or an orderly nuclear attack. Adjectives aside, it was still cancer.

After the diagnostic phone call from Dr. Schaitkin, I felt I had taken my first step—one I hoped would lead to a quick journey to recovery. I had explained to Dr. Schaitkin how I had arrived at the answer but was frustrated because no one was listening. And to top it off, the MRI before my unnecessary surgery had turned up negative.

"Send me the film," he said.

I put the bulky package of films in the mail to Pittsburgh and waited patiently for days. Waiting is difficult when your life might hang in the balance. It seemed interminable, but five days later, Dr. Schaitkin called.

"Sorry for the delay, and keep in mind I'm not a radiologist, but I was unhappy at the way the scan was done. I've been carrying the film around here and getting different opinions," he told me. "The consensus is that there really was no proper scan of the parotid—just a cursory review. They couldn't have found anything with that."

The apparent acquiescence of the radiology staff to my insistence on having a parotid scan that day in New York had all been a charade—a way to get the annoying patient to shut up and get him out of the office. It was an inadequate, incomplete, and halfheartedly done test.

"You need another MRI scan," Dr. Schaitkin told me from Pittsburgh. "A 3-D scan with thinner cuts."

"Really?" I thought to myself, recalling my earlier unsuccessful efforts to get an MRI done with precisely the same technique. I was starting to like this guy even more.

I boarded a USAir 737 in a buoyant mood on a frigid February morning for the one-hour-and-fifteen-minute flight to Pittsburgh. My impression didn't change after I met Barry Schaitkin at the University of Pittsburgh Medical Center in Shadyside, on the city's leafy east side. We hit it off instantly, bound in some way, I think, by our marvel at how intransigent and closed-minded the experts had been about other opinions, especially that of a lowly patient.

As we settled into his comfortable but rather Spartan office, he reached behind himself and pulled a book from the shelf above his desk. It was *The Facial Nerve*, considered the seminal textbook in the field, which he had coauthored with Mark May. He took a step around the desk, opened the book, and pointed to a line he had written years before.

"An incomplete facial paralysis that fails to improve within a few months is caused by a tumor until proved otherwise."

I thought briefly of the succession of specialists so keen on Bell's palsy. I read the line again with a hint of vindication, not anger. We talked briefly about my self-diagnosis, but we were there to move ahead and get started on treatment, not revisit and overanalyze the past. The next step was an MRI. "I'm impressed, Dr. Iqbal. Your logic and reasoning are quite focused," he told me.

"I've done more thinking and have come up with something else," I said. "I'm sure the tumor is located in the deeper layers of the parotid, and I'm fairly certain that it is small, under two centimeters."

"OK, Sherlock," he said, smiling, "how do you know this?"

I played along. "Elementary, my dear Watson, the tumor has to be in the deeper layer; otherwise, I'd be able to feel it on the surface. I can't." I continued, "And the tumor first grabbed the upper two branches of the facial nerve and then, after a few months, the next two, still sparing the lowest one—which means it is sitting near the bifurcation of the nerve, which is a distance of only a centimeter, which means it's only one to two centimeters wide."

"Makes perfect sense," he said, smiling approvingly as we got up and headed for MRI. Someone was finally listening to me. I'll admit it felt great and helped boost my confidence that my detective work had indeed led me to the correct diagnosis.

Using the 3-D technology and the thinner slices I had asked for months earlier in New Jersey, that is exactly what it showed. I drew a quick breath when I saw the tumor on the scan. The enemy at last was in sight, and it momentarily frightened me, this quarry I'd been looking for so long, this tiny gray shadow that wanted to kill me—no bigger than a fingernail, yet so deadly. It was a stark reminder, but the apprehension passed and my resolve returned.

"Let's take care of this," I said.

Back in his office, Dr. Schaitkin outlined his recommendations for treatment, reminding me that as rare as they are, less than 1% of all cancers, the vast majority of malignant parotid tumors were easily treatable. "Long term, the outlook is good." Any cancer discussion with a doctor that involves the phrase *long term* is a good one.

I was lucky, or so I thought. The vast majority of parotid cancers are not particularly aggressive. My tumor was small. The prognosis for recovery was good. But the surgery to remove the tumor and any possible tissue in the complicated facial landscape where it could have spread—called a radical parotidectomy—was not for the faint of heart, nor for the vain. There was nothing gentle about it. It would cut nerves, slice tendons, and remove flesh. It was an extensive and disfiguring surgery, much like the radical mastectomy for breast cancer.

Dr. Schaitkin and the University of Pittsburgh Medical Center staff remained true to form—unshakable, optimistic, and confident. They were prepared to choreograph the delicate surgery to remove the tumor and surrounding tissue and then apply the latest plastic surgery techniques to help me leave Pittsburgh with the tumor gone and my face reconstructed.

Removing any tumor is complicated, even if it is as small as mine was. Any surrounding tissue would have to go as well, on the chance that the malignancy had spread to lymph nodes and beyond. Microscopic and potentially lethal bits of the tumor would not show on a scan until they grew, and by then, it could be too late. He explained how they would first remove the soft tissue, all the flesh, from the left side of my face, leaving nothing but skin and bones. The process included removing the facial nerve itself and then moving farther out to the upper part of my neck, where a dissection would remove further tissue. It was not going to be pretty. And after all this facial excavation, the now nerveless left side of my face would sag flaccidly, skin without support.

Once that was done and the wound had healed, I'd be bombarded with radiation. None of this was a surprise. I knew and expected that much.

I was surprised, though, by the fact that the medical center specialized in facial reconstruction after the demolition of surgeries like mine—their thinking being that a patient, after such a devastating surgery, should have at least some semblance of normalcy. I liked the thought that I would not have to wait to have my face rebuilt, that I would not have to walk around looking as if the left side of my face had somehow melted, as if it were nothing but skin and bone. I would never again have a functioning facial nerve. The left half of my face will never regain the ability to smile or express any emotions. But, at least, I would have some semblance of a facial contour.

Dr. Schaitkin knew I was heading right back to New Jersey that afternoon, and he arranged for a meeting that morning with plastic surgeon Bill Schwartz, who graciously invited me right over to his office.

As part of the facial nerve team, Dr. Schwartz had become an expert in postparotidectomy reconstruction.

He explained what I thought were my three options. The first was to remove a tendon from my forearm and plant it in the left side of my face to act as a hook to pull up the corner of my lips; the second was to take a muscle from my groin and implant it in my face to give it contour; and the third was to remove a long section of nerve from my calf, cut it into four pieces, and implant it in my face in place of the various branches of facial nerve and hope it might serve as a good substitute.

It was a bit overwhelming, all this talk of cutting and sewing and rebuilding. "Do you want me to decide which of those three you should do?" I asked.

"Oh no, not at all. We will do all three. The chance of success for any of them is so poor we always have to do all three for better odds."

Somewhat stunned by the extent of corrective surgery and the mention of the poor success rate, my only response was to meekly mutter, "Oh, I see."

I told Dr. Schaitkin I thought I should go to Memorial Sloan Kettering in New York City and have the surgery done there. It was certainly not a reflection on the wonderful people I met at Pittsburgh but rather more of my inclination to stay close to home, and Sloan was, after all, the preeminent cancer facility in the country. One would think after my previous meetings filled with preeminence—the surgeons and the hospitals of the past ten months—that I might have had had enough of preeminence, that I might be leaning instead more toward competence and concern.

I was not—even after all I'd been through. Dr. Schaitkin was fine with that. The pieces were now in place. My next struggle was to break the news to my family.

I walked outside Shadyside into the brisk Pittsburgh air to meet my sister-in-law Rakhshanda, who had met me at the airport and would take me back.

"So what happened?" she asked.

"They found the tumor."

I watched her eyes searching my face for signs of panic or maybe even despair.

"But it's not malignant, right?" she asked.

"Yes. It is malignant."

She was confused. "But you are not talking about cancer, right?"

"Yes, it is cancer."

Rakhshanda started to cry. "Why are you so calm then?"

"Because we'll take care of it. It's a good sign they found it, and we will now take care of it," I said, adding, "Just do me a favor and don't call Fauzia until I tell her myself."

At the airport, I called Sheeraz, who was about to graduate from medical school, and I told him to get started on researching parotid tumors.

"Let's see what we can learn—we must learn as much as we can."

Sheeraz seemed to take strength from my calmness. "Not a problem. I'll get started right away and have some information printed out for you by the time you get back home."

Fauzia met me at the door, looking tentative and nervous. I again reassured her all was well, that in fact we were in a good place. I explained what was about to happen and how we were on the way to recovery. I emphasized the positive.

"It's the undiagnosed cancer that was the worst part, my love," I told her.

We looked at each other, knowing we would be facing a challenge unlike anything else we'd been through. But we knew we would be doing it together, unified in strength and buoyed by the knowledge that things could be worse. We drew hope from Dr. Schaitkin's optimistic assessment that it was treatable and had a good prognosis.

I felt we would go into this together, without too much fear. And all would be well.

I was unable to schedule an appointment at Memorial Sloan Kettering until February 14, when I would meet with its top authority on head and neck surgery. As I always did, I arrived early for the appointment, and as always happened, I still waited for two hours before I saw the doctor.

Almost immediately, the discussion took a different direction from the rosier path Barry Schaitkin and the staff at Pittsburgh had laid out. The doctor had by then viewed the enhanced scans from Pittsburgh and told me he agreed with the diagnosis. I had a malignant tumor, and he would remove it. But, he said, he was not interested in reconstructive surgery, nor did he think it was an appropriate measure.

"Why not?" I asked.

"Dr. Iqbal, you realize that your life is in serious danger, don't you?" he said in a businesslike tone—absent of anything that could be construed as empathy. This was the first mention in all those months of death, of the ultimate challenge.

"All I am concerned with at this point is saving your life. We can worry about cosmetic surgery in a couple of years," he continued. What he had meant, perhaps, in his officious and efficient statement was "Let's take care of the tumor first."

What I heard was something quite different. "Why get involved in cosmetic surgery until we find out if you'll even live long enough to make it worthwhile? Why waste our time?" It was as if he had stood up from behind his desk and hit me with a baseball bat. I was not prepared for that. I had not gone down that road, but there he was, pushing me right along a path I had deliberately chosen to ignore.

You might not survive.

It was an ominous prognosis to say the least. I recovered quickly and looked him straight in the eye. "Well, I plan to live a full life after the cancer. And I want a reconstructed face while I live that long life."

We were miles apart in our thinking. He shrugged. I stood, offered my thanks, and shook his hand. "I think I'll go back to Pittsburgh," I said.

At this moment, it seems nothing is left
Neither moon, nor sun, neither darkness, nor dawn

The eyes behold a veiled vision of beauty
While anguish resides in the sanctuaries of my heart

Perhaps a hallucination, perhaps I did hear
Footsteps in the streets of a final walk

In the branches of the dense tree of my thoughts
No dream shall come to nest anymore

No amity, no enmity, no connection, no relation
Neither a friend of yours, nor a stranger of mine

True, this desolate moment is immensely difficult
But it is, my heart, just one moment after all
Be courageous, there is a lifetime yet to live.

This poem (translated by the author) is by Faiz Ahmed Faiz, a famous Urdu poet. He wrote it while in an intensive care unit struggling for his life. He lived.

CHAPTER 9

IT IS ONLY ONE MOMENT

February 2002

The car was still warm in the garage after my Valentine's Day denouement with the doctor at Sloan when I phoned Barry Schaitkin.

"I'm coming back," I told him.

I turned confidently to Pittsburgh and Dr. Schaitkin's team in Shadyside, vibrantly aware of the seriousness of the surgery I was about to submit to but calm as always. I knew confidence was contagious, and I spread the message to my family with the fervency of an evangelist.

"Yes, it is serious. I'm having major surgery. Yes, I will have fairly prolonged radiation treatment that will leave me drained and exhausted. Yes, it will be a bit of a tough road. But so what? Once I am cancer-free, I will put it all behind me and we'll go on as planned, with Sheeraz's June wedding as a great target for a clean bill of health. Most parotid cancers are of a gentler type," I would tell them. "They are easy to treat. I will not have to face debilitating rounds of chemotherapy. The surgery and radiation treatments offer a great chance for a long and normal life."

Things moved quickly, and by Tuesday, February 19, Fauzia and I were on yet another USAir flight to Pittsburgh for the surgery that would cure me of cancer and save my life, or so I hoped.

Sheeraz, who was finishing medical school, Noreen, a student at NYU, and Daniyal, who was only twelve, would follow us to Pittsburgh, making the 360-mile drive the next day to be there when I went in for surgery. I felt my optimism and encouragement had put everyone in the proper state of mind, though I did harbor some worry about how Fauzia was processing all this new and frightening information.

Sympathy and support poured in from every corner of our extended family and community of friends. Sheeraz's future in-laws, who had already put down a sizable deposit for the wedding reception at Brooklyn Botanical Gardens, said they would be willing to lose it if we wanted to postpone the wedding. I would have none of that. The wedding would go on as planned, and I would dance joyfully at the reception. It was as simple as that. Despite my immense optimism, there was a nagging little fear in the back of my mind that, if the wedding got postponed, I might not live to see that special day.

At 7:00 a.m. on Thursday, February 21, 2002, with my family and my good medical school friend Mehboob, who had made the cross-state drive from Allentown, at my side, I stepped into the lobby of Shadyside Medical Center and into the good hands of what would prove to be an astonishingly able crew. The staff, from the orderlies who wheeled my gurney to the top surgeons, was nothing short of amazing.

"Is there anything else I can help you with?" seemed to be a consistent refrain, a mantra upheld by seemingly all of the staff.

It would be a long day, with surgeons estimating the surgery to excise the cancer, followed by a second and delicate reconstruction, could be as long as twelve hours. "I'll see you later," I told the nervous group as they rolled me into the operating theater. For me, of course, under and out, the actual eleven hours it took to finish were like the blink of an eye. For my family and Mehboob, it must have seemed interminable. In keeping with the mindfulness they practiced, the hospital staff provided frequent updates, something that was quite unusual at the time in most hospitals.

After about six hours of tense and nerve-racking waiting, my family received the news that the cancer surgery had been successful and the reconstruction had started. Everyone relaxed enough now to move to a nearby hotel suite Mehboob had reserved for the day. Fauzia and the kids tried to rest—or at least appear to be resting—but the day dragged on. Even catnaps proved difficult for all of them.

Afterward, I was moved to the recovery room and a few hours later into the intensive care unit, where I would stay for two days.

I woke up groggy and wrapped in a mental fog Friday morning. My first thought, surprising me, was "Thank God I'm still alive." I had taken such pains to assure everyone of the relative lack of danger that I had buried thoughts of my own mortality. But there it was. Somewhere in the back of my mind, I had suppressed the thought that I might not survive, just barely scratching the surface of my consciousness.

When I awoke, happy to be alive, soaking in the light and noise, I was not exactly comfortable. I had an irritating breathing tube inserted, which precluded me from speaking. I looked down to see various lines running into my arms, one was patient-controlled analgesia, or PCA, which was an IV drip with a button I could push that injected quick bursts of painkillers when I felt the need.

As the day progressed, my face swelled rapidly and my blood count for hemoglobin dropped dramatically. I had quickly become anemic, and it was clear that I was bleeding internally. I did not know then but would learn later that during reconstruction a suture used to connect a vein from my left ankle to a facial artery had come undone. As the hemoglobin dropped lower and lower and close to dangerous levels, I grew increasingly concerned and had what may have outwardly appeared to be a comical reaction. I began writing frantic notes to Mehboob.

"I want another hemoglobin, STAT."

"I have an uncontrolled internal bleeding."

"I want this fixed ASAP. Call Dr. Schwartz."

"I want a blood transfusion, STAT!"

"What is taking so long?"

Of course, the surgical team and the staff were completely on top of the issue, and there was absolutely no chance they had overlooked anything. I was in good hands. What was remarkable was that, somehow, they tolerated my excessive note-writing and backseat doctoring.

My family still teases me about that. And I suppose I deserve it.

Yet there was reason to be concerned. My hemoglobin count was alarmingly low at approximately 6.5 grams per deciliter. The normal range is between 12 and 16. My own was usually about 16 grams per deciliter. There was a great deal of uncontrolled bleeding, and I began to worry legitimately that I might die if it was not stopped. Looking back, I don't think my life was ever in imminent danger. My fears might have been unfounded, but the panic was real.

And then my thoughts drifted once more, a function of the strong pain medication more than my own normal thought patterns. "If the excessive bleeding continues," I told myself, "I will go into a state of medical shock, where my pulse will dim and my heart rate will slow until I faint. It would be a peaceful way to go," I thought, "and I would not suffer much." The logic was oddly comforting, and I began to calm down.

Instead of resigning myself, though, I asked for another transfusion, which quickly brought my hemoglobin count back up.

It took almost four hours of additional surgery to control the bleeding and to drain the large amount of blood that had escaped from the broken suture.

I was returned to intensive care where I dropped into a fragile state, engulfed in a stupor the likes of which I had never experienced. My face, which had now been the site of two radical surgeries, was bruised and swollen. For the rest of Friday and all day Saturday, I drifted in and out of consciousness. I had never been so sick in my entire life.

I knew then my situation was desperate, and for the second time in as many days, I thought of my own mortality, unfamiliar territory to be sure. I didn't know if I would make it.

Fauzia spent the entire three days at my bedside, taking comfort in the exceptional kindness of the nurses. One caring nurse brought her a wool blanket to ward off the hospital-room chill and gave her an encouraging squeeze.

"He'll be fine," she said.

Because I was in a stupor most of the time, I was mostly oblivious to Fauzia's presence. But Noreen noticed that I tended to become restless if Fauzia left my side for too long.

Sheeraz kept things running as smoothly as possible, consulting with the doctors and nurses while shepherding Daniyal and Noreen in for quick visits. Mehboob left Friday, replaced on the caring visitors' roster Saturday by Javed and Wanda, who flew in from New Jersey. Fauzia's sister and brother-in-law were stalwarts, on constant call from nearby Latrobe.

All the while, I remained in a twilight zone of sorts, drifting in and out, a famous Urdu poem from one of the master poets of his time, if not of all time, Faiz Ahmad Faiz repeatedly running through my mind. No stranger to turmoil himself, Faiz had written it on what he thought might be his deathbed.

> I acknowledge that this desolate moment
> Is the most difficult to endure
> But it is, after all, just one moment
> Be brave, my heart
> There's a lifetime yet to live

He survived, and so would I.

When my head finally began to clear, I realized I had taken great strength from those words. Faiz was a poet of immense internal strength, a man who had gone through hellish trials but had never given up. His poetry was a defiant celebration of faith, not of darkness or complaint.

I would stay strong because I had a long life ahead.

By Sunday, the crisis had passed and I was transferred from the ICU to a floor of regular patients. Dr. Schaitkin had visited and told me he was pleased with the cancer surgery and was awaiting only the pathology results before he'd send me to Rakhshanda's in Latrobe on Tuesday and then home to begin my recovery and radiation treatments.

On Tuesday, Dr. Schaitkin dropped by my room and I knew immediately from the look on his face that something was not right. He pulled a chair next to the recliner where I had been sitting, a wool blanket across my lap. "Look," he said, taking a deep breath, "I have some bad news."

I caught my own breath as my heart seemed to skip a few beats.

"The pathology report shows your cancer is not the common one we had hoped for, the one we had planned our post-op treatment around. It is not the gentle kind."

"What do you mean?" I asked.

"Sajjad, it is salivary duct carcinoma, an extremely rare parotid cancer that is exceptionally malignant and aggressive."

"And the stage?" I almost whispered.

"Between III and IV."

My head started spinning.

Parotid cancers are very rare, less than one percent of all cancers. There are several histological types, the vast majority being easily treated and offering a good prognosis. But the rarest of all— as rare as one in a million—is salivary duct carcinoma. It is an extremely malignant cancer with a poor prognosis.

All cancers can be classified into four stages. Stage I is the earliest form when the cancer is small and well confined inside an organ. Stage II cancer means the tumor has grown but is still contained. Stage III means the cancer has attacked other structures outside the organ from which it started. Stage IV means the cancer has spread to distant organs or lymph nodes.

So, I had the worst type of cancer that had already advanced substantially. My heart fluttered as I tried to absorb the enormity of what I'd just been told.

My mantra of hope, my glorification of optimism, and my stalwart defense of the rosy path back to health were all gone in that instant. I sat paralyzed, my mind running in too many directions simultaneously. I tried to catch my breath, but I was not up to the challenge.

"Look, we've removed all traces of this cancer. That's why I was so optimistic after the surgery when I spoke to you on Sunday. But this is the type of cancer that almost always comes back. And it could come back in the same general area or in some distant parts of the body. It is vicious. And it's unpredictable."

I stared ahead as he continued, "You will need very aggressive treatment, and I am recommending chemotherapy in addition to the radiation."

I pulled the blanket from my lap and dropped it on the floor beside me. I was no longer chilled. I felt nothing. I continued to sit, stunned, trying to take in the enormity of what he was saying, my imagined walk in the park now a projected death march, perhaps. My head reeled, but my analytical self slowly began to take charge again. Momentarily stunned, I pulled myself back together.

"OK, now what do we do?" I asked. I knew enough at that point to understand that chemotherapy had in the past been ineffective in treating parotid cancers.

"We still have to be aggressive with the radiation," he told me. "But this cancer is so mean we're going to have to throw the kitchen sink at it. We are going to use everything we have in our arsenal."

"But chemo?" I asked again.

"Look. Some of the chemo treatments for parotid cancers in those studies were done over thirty years ago. No one has tried chemotherapy since. We have newer chemotherapy drugs, and we should try them. Who knows? New drugs just might work. True, there is no evidence that modern chemo works better for your cancer. But there is also no evidence that it does not. We should try it."

As with everything he did, Dr. Schaitkin took my schedule and my obvious shock into consideration and arranged for me to see an oncologist that afternoon. The future had taken on a new urgency.

Fauzia and her sister picked me up at Shadyside, and I gave them only the barest of explanations for my sudden need to head over to Montefiore Hospital across town to see the oncologist, Dr. Chin. "A slight complication," was all I said.

Dr. Chin agreed with Dr. Schaitkin's recommendations in every respect—radiation and chemo together, simultaneously.

"Even though there are no data on the effectiveness of chemo with this type of aggressive cancer," Dr. Chin told me, "I think this might help and I think we should try it." Then came the inevitable question.

"What is my prognosis?" I asked him, trying to sound casual.

"Thirty percent."

I went immediately to the standard translations of that figure, 30 percent chance of survival for a certain number of years, usually five.

"Do you mean 30 percent chance of surviving for five years?" I asked, taking no comfort from those odds.

"No. Two years. We really don't have data on five-year survival with this cancer."

"Oh my God," I thought. "That means practically no one survives five years."

That was it, the final blow to my quickly eroding optimism. I was devastated. They didn't expect me to live two years. I would see Sheeraz's wedding but not those of my other children and would likely not live long enough to become a grandfather. Complete devastation overcame me.

My life compressed in that tsunami of a comment. "Two years," I thought, "and even that is not likely. Only a 30 percent chance!"

I sat there, momentarily dumbstruck, and then I said, "OK. We'll do chemo as well as radiation."

However, this course of action was such a radical departure from the standard clinical practice that I wanted to go home and get more opinions.

Somehow the light that had been so radically snuffed out by this chaotic afternoon of bad news showed signs of life again, a flicker of hope.

As I was leaving Dr. Chin's office, my thoughts turned to baseball, my favorite sport. Thirty percent? You want a player who's hitting .300 at the plate when the game is on line.

The .300 hitters are great hitters; it's tough to get them out. I started liking my chances a bit more. If I'm a .300 hitter, I've got a good chance of surviving.

More than anything, I wanted to survive.

Forget about two years or five years or some vague statistical threat. I wanted to live. I would live one day at a time. That was my new mantra.

It had been one hell of an afternoon.

By then, the children and Javed and Wanda had returned to New Jersey, all thinking everything was under control. On the drive back to Latrobe, I told Fauzia and Rakhshanda and her husband Shahid a bit more of the darker news.

"Complications," I said. "There are always complications. But I will be fine."

I had decided to continue my facade of easy grace, but my nerves were taut. I trotted out my baseball analogy, but those three people so dear to me sat in stunned silence.

They didn't seem to be buying it. When we got to their house, Rakhshanda put on some music videos to distract us. To this day, I can't tell you who it was or even hum the tune, but one video on screen made me freeze. It was a happy family singing an upbeat tune—a mother and a father and their two adorable children gleeful, merry, all professing their love for each other and their unsullied togetherness. They would love each other and be together forever, they sang.

Immediately, I identified myself with that father and my family with that family in the music video. And then came the crushing reminder of my own impending mortality and that my beautiful family had little chance of staying happily and lovingly together forever and ever.

Hope drained from me as the song ended. Baseball analogies and mantras of optimism vaporized, and I lost control, sobbing openly and unapologetically for the first time in years.

I could not let go of the image of that happy family, which in many ways seemed like my own. I realized then that my life was precious and my time left to enjoy it precarious.

I would not live forever.

CHAPTER 10
A DANCE OF JOY

June 2002

I made it, just as I had planned and hoped.

From the day I received the devastating news that I had cancer with a subsequent death sentence attached, I had set this day, Sheeraz's wedding, as my first baby step of achievement. I had to survive long enough to see my first child, my first son, get married. There would be no stopping me, and here I was.

I did it.

Away from the hustle and bustle of Manhattan, we gathered in the idyllic sanctuary of Brooklyn's Botanical Gardens. On that surprisingly pleasant June evening, the garden was not only a riot of rich colors and crisp fragrances, but also an animated play that unfolded in the most beautiful wedding, right before my eyes.

Dark, luxuriant green trees stood tall around us in celebration of Sheeraz and Reem's union. Stunning sunflowers stretched in the cool breeze as guests wrote best wishes on pretty little silk ribbons and tied them on a Mexican sun-flower tree blooming in its full glory. I watched the colorful ribbons flutter against the yellow and green of the tree, as if silently singing prayers for the couple. Reem walked in, on the arm of her beaming father, wearing a stunning white gown with a long and flowing train. She looked like a beau-tiful fairy princess right out of every little girl's dreams. Three bridesmaids walked behind Reem, guiding her train and straightening her dress as well as they could until she reached Sheeraz. He kissed the back of her hand.

Sheeraz looked incredibly handsome and elegant in a stylish deep-blue Armani suit. Together, they made a per-fect couple. I was bursting with pride for Sheeraz, my hard-working firstborn son, who was entering a new phase of his life, having just graduated and become a doctor. And now at his side was his beautiful bride, Reem, an able partner who had also fallen in love with medicine and was training to be an internist.

I sat next to my lovely wife, Fauzia, who looked abso-lutely radiant in a shimmery dusty-gold silk sari, her red-dish-blond hair so meticulously coiffed. In contrast to her delicate beauty, I looked horrendous. The entire left half of my face was paralyzed, drooping, and practically blackened from the recent intense radiation treatment. Any attempt to smile pulled my lips all the way to the right side, greatly exaggerating the facial asymmetry.

I had lost a lot of weight. My suit hung loosely on my small frame as if I had borrowed it from an older brother. I had been through hell, and it showed. Normally, I weighed about 130 to 135 pounds, and at 120 pounds, I feared that onlookers could tell how frail I had grown. I clutched

Fauzia's hand as Sheeraz proclaimed his love for Reem. Voice quivering with emotion, he said, "I waited so long for this. I never thought I would be lucky enough to see this day."

With tears in her eyes, Reem responded, "If somebody told me I would fall in love with a man so kind, gentle, and sweet and he would love me back just as intensely, I would have never believed him."

Silently, I echoed their emotions. I was so happy I had survived to see this day.

I have to admit I was bursting with pride in myself as well. The four months leading up to the wedding were not easy. But I had set my sights and I had made it, against all odds. And the fact of the matter was, I didn't just sit passively at the wedding like the limp survivor of some sort of ritualistic torture—which in many ways my cancer treatment had been. Rather, I relished every single moment and every guest in attendance. I dove headlong into the festivities, and as anyone who has attended a traditional Pakistani wedding knows, that takes a great deal of energy.

These weddings are three-day affairs that hold little back. They are not for the faint of heart.

Friday night, before the main Saturday ceremony at the stunning Brooklyn Botanical Gardens, guests had gathered in New Jersey for the colorful *mehndi* ceremony, the ritual painting of the bride's hands with henna—a ceremony thousands of years old, meant to provide the bride with good luck, health, and sensuality. Everyone at the large gathering was dressed elegantly and festively, in clothes that exploded with color.

Fauzia, a master event planner, had everything organized, including a wonderful band thumping the beat of traditional Pakistani music, with a vocalist singing popular wedding songs that had everyone joining in, including me. There was plenty of food laid out on long tables on two sides of the dance floor, with white-clad caterers dishing out delicacies, such as chicken tikka, kabab, korma, lamb chops, biryani, and so much more.

We danced late into the night, and I heard a familiar comment from many of the guests who watched me. "Where did you get that energy?"

I wondered myself. Only a few days earlier, I had finished my last radiation treatment, and I was exhausted. I was not a pretty sight to be sure, but I could have danced all night and sung to boot. It felt like pure adrenaline.

That was my first appearance in front of many friends and acquaintances who knew that I had been undergoing the rigorous chemotherapy and radiation treatments but had not seen me for months. When I was not in treatment, I was resting or working. Those four months for me were not a time for socializing. They were painful, frankly, and debilitating—nothing to brush aside. I had to remain focused to get through it so that I could make it to the wedding.

We headed to Brooklyn the next day with hardly any sleep, ready for the main ceremony—the wedding itself. On the drive over, I realized for the first time, adrenaline subsiding, that I had overdone it the night before. Despite this, I would not have changed a thing. I was ready for what turned out to be a beautiful and romantic wedding in a picture-perfect setting. It was touching. As anyone who has ever watched a child marry would recognize, I felt a bittersweet mix of nostalgia for the baby I remembered and joy at the man he had become.

But I was fatigued and at one point not too long after the ceremony, when the dancing and music started up again, I had no strength to recreate my zest from the night before. I slipped away for a nap in the waiting limo.

A Pakistani wedding is in many ways a triathlon, and it requires endurance, pacing, and strategic breaks along the way to make it to the finish line. Sunday was another reception, the *walima*, the groom's reception, which, not surprisingly, continued the joy and the music and the food of the first two days.

When I look back on it, what I recall the most was my miraculous energy, a real gift from above.

There is no way around the simple fact that cancer is an ugly disease and treating it is equally ugly.

If a disinterested person were to look at wedding photos from that weekend, his or her eyes would be pulled to the thin man with the disfigured face smiling back at the camera, like rubberneckers gawking at a gruesome highway accident.

But they would not see the full picture. First, I was smiling in every photo, every single one of the many that were snapped over that long weekend. I could not stop smiling even though I knew it distorted my face even further. I was in the pictures, and that was all that mattered. My smiles were nothing more than a reflection of my joy in my son's good fortune. They were sweet smiles of victory. But they did not tell the whole story of the four months that got me there.

Before the treatments began, I had set a simple goal: I will defy the odds. I will attend the wedding. I will go through this, and I will be there—that is the prize.

A few years after this trying experience, we had a friend named Arjan, who had been diagnosed with cancer and was about to begin chemotherapy. His wife, a dear friend for decades, Neelam, had called me in tears, wanting to know what would happen, how things would unfold. Fauzia discouraged me from telling them the gritty details, but I thought that giving lip service to this heinous but ultimately life-saving process would do him no good at all. Should I simply tell him not to worry, that it would be fine, and it was not so bad? I didn't think so.

He was afraid—afraid of the pain and the suffering and everything he had heard about chemotherapy treatments. "You should be," I confided. "Your fears are valid."

So I told him, in great and perhaps depressing detail, what I had gone through. And I think that helped him immensely. I pulled no punches. "It will not be a picnic," I told my friend. "In fact, it will be horrible and lengthy and push you to the edge of despair. But in the end, the reward for the pain and debilitation and exhaustion will be life. There is no greater gift than that. Take comfort in the millions of people who have gone through this and survived," I shared. "Take strength from knowing you are not alone and you are not the first person to go through this. Enduring cancer treatments is not a matter of heroics." I told him what I had told Sheeraz shortly before I started my own treatments. "Imagine you are on the second floor of a house that is engulfed in flames. You have only one way out if you want to survive, jumping though a broken window forty feet up and into the flames. There will be no net to cushion your fall. You know you'll be cut by shards of glass, scraped and banged and burned as you pass through the jagged opening. You know when you land you might break an arm or a leg and be in great pain. You know also, though, that you will have escaped the inferno and a horrible death. You know you will mend and move on. I have to say that I was horribly sick for months, but I will quickly add I would go through the same things again if necessary."

I can't say that I consoled my friend, but I was honest with him. Sometimes you need a friend to just tell it like it is, and on that day, that was my duty. It's almost like a secret society; you're in a club nobody else knows about until they too have cancer. But once you're in the club, you help one another in every way possible because you're not just fighting your own battle; you're part of a bigger fight, a huge war being fought in cities, states, and countries around the world.

My friend took it all to heart. With his devoted wife, Neelam, by his side, he gallantly fought this deadly enemy and bravely endured the unbearable side effects. He triumphed. As I write this, he has been cancer free for eighteen months and looks every bit as healthy as ever before.

My thoughts drifted back to my own battle and the news I had received from Dr. Schaitkin, announcing mine was the most aggressive type of cancer. The evening in Latrobe was sad and difficult, but it passed.

By the time I was back home, I had adopted my batting average analogy as my mantra.

Why couldn't I be among the 30 percent who beat this? But I had a decision to make while I was stepping up to the plate, and I wanted to discuss it with others before I moved on. The chemo and radiation combination recommended by Dr. Schaitkin and his oncologist Dr. Chin was a new approach at the time. The parotid cancers, even salivary duct carcinoma, had always been treated with surgery and then heavy doses of radiation. There was little data available to indicate whether adding the chemotherapy worked any better.

The medical community is conservative by nature and does not easily accept anything considered new or radically different from the accepted standard. I was part of that community, I suppose, because I went back to Sloan for a consultation.

The doctor there was emphatically against adding chemo to my treatment regimen. "There is absolutely no evidence it will help," he said, "and the only thing I can guarantee to you if you decide to add chemo is that you will be miserable."

I even called an expert in salivary gland cancers at Johns Hopkins. I told her my situation and asked her whether I should try chemo with the radiation.

"No," she said. "There are too many side effects and nothing to show that it works."

"Let me ask you this," I said to her after her pronouncement. "What would you say my prognosis is?"

The momentary silence on the other end was broken as I heard her take a deep breath. This was a physician talking to a colleague. There would be no sugarcoated response, just a single word.

"Poor."

Even though I was expecting that, it threw me for a loop as I slumped back in my favorite chair. Once again, I turned to my laptop to research more that evening. There was no time left for waffling or self-pity. In front of my computer as evening became the wee hours of the morning, I was frozen by two lines that jumped from the screen. I won't forget them.

"Salivary duct carcinoma is among the most aggressive and malignant tumors in the body. Most patients die within two years despite treatment."

"*Most* patients," I thought. So much for batting .300.

It hit me like a sudden and violent punch to my heart. So often I had heard that phrase, "felt like a punch to my heart." That night, for the first time ever, I knew exactly what it meant.

No one wants to die, of course. My thoughts were drawn to my family and things I would miss if I were gone. Here I was, fifty-four years old with a loving wife and wonderful kids and a bright future ahead of me if I could beat this. That was my motivator. I would beat this thing. I would triumph. I had no choice.

All of it, the life I would miss, flashed by in a torrent of emotions. "I want to live," I thought. "I want to watch my children grown into successful adults, to see my grandchildren, to play with them. I want to be with Fauzia and age gracefully with her. I don't want Fauzia to be alone."

Sheeraz and I were so close to our long-held dream of sharing a practice, of me eventually stepping aside and giving him the reins of what I had started. He had three years of residency left before we could complete our mission—father and son practicing side by side.

"At the very least, I have to make it three years," I thought.

Those grim words in that textbook were all I needed to decide to go with chemotherapy as well as radiation. The consensus was that people with salivary duct carcinoma had a very high rate of relapse. If I went through the standard radiation treatment alone and the cancer returned, I would kick myself. I'd second-guess myself right into oblivion. Would it have come back if I had done the chemo as well? No, I could not take that risk. After this epiphany, there was no longer any doubt. I would be going all in.

Dr. Chin had been frank when I asked about complications. There would be vomiting, nausea, and inability to eat driven by loss of appetite and the mouth riddled with painful sores. I might need surgery to allow for a tube feeding directly into my stomach because the radiation would wreak havoc on my mouth and throat. There would be muscle pain, joint pain, and severe bone pain. I might become too weak to get out of bed. My blood count would drop, and I would become anemic. I would not be able to fight even the feeblest infection. The radical bombardment of my body from the chemicals and the radiation would weaken my heart and lungs. I would lose my hair. The list just went on and on.

"Fine," I thought. "I will deal with it, this vile enemy, but I will not make concessions."

"I still want to continue to work," I told Dr. Chin.

"You might be able to pull it off for the first two weeks," Dr. Chin replied. "But after that, you will become progressively sicker and weaker. I doubt you'll have enough strength to do much other than getting your treatment and going home to rest."

"I will find the strength. I *will* keep working." I silently made this vow to myself as I left his office.

I visited a local oncologist whom I had known professionally and discussed my situation. He agreed to prescribe and administer the chemotherapy based upon the regimen for breast cancer.

Beginning April 8, 2002, I would have six weeks of chemotherapy along with what would later prove to be nine weeks of radiation. That would be enough, and I would be finished in time to recover a bit for Sheeraz's wedding in June.

I called Mehboob, my internist friend, and told him what I was doing and that I was planning to keep working as well. He chuckled. "Are you kidding me? You will be taking both Taxol and Carboplatin plus radiation, and you want to keep working? You'll be lucky if you can get out of bed."

My brother Javed agreed with my friend and tried to convince me to hire a physician to take over my practice while I was in treatment. He even offered to pay for it and left me a blank check. Grateful as I was, that did not appeal to me at all. No concessions.

And so it began. I scheduled my chemotherapy sessions at the nearby Valley Hospital in Ridgewood, a short drive from home. I'd go there every Tuesday for the five-hour process, along with Fauzia, who never left my side. For the guest of honor, the process involves one thing, patience. I sat for five hours in a comfortable recliner while these various cancer killers seeped into my body. For me, it was Taxol and Carboplatin after intravenous combinations of other substances meant to reduce side effects, such as the vomiting that would come later.

With me in the large and comfortably lit room were others undergoing their own rituals, which provided a sense of community—of knowing that I was not alone. I would not wish the process on my worst enemy, but knowing that others were facing the same fears and feeling the same side effects was comforting and familiar for me. We were allies on the front of a war against this horrible disease. Fauzia and I became close with a woman fighting breast cancer, and we tried to help her find some sense of comfort as she suffered through side effects.

Most of the time, I would simply fall asleep. It became something of a running joke with the staff, who would set up my drips and then as they walked away, whisper, "Nighty night."

I was confident by then that I was doing as much as I could. I had left nothing to chance. Knowing that allowed me to appear confident. That was half the game right there. I brought with me Lance Armstrong's book, *It's Not about the Bike*, his frank and fascinating story about his own cancer battle. At the time, Armstrong was a world-class athlete on his way to winning an astounding seventh Tour de France, perhaps the most grueling sporting challenge. Though his victories were later discredited, what he had done to beat cancer was nothing short of inspiring. As his testicular cancer spread, he was literally hours from death at one point. Yet he did not give up hope, and he beat it. His story is heroic in the truest sense of the word. His battle and his determination inspired tens of thousands of other cancer patients, including me. I was awed by his determination and felt I needed to have whatever it was that pulled him out of it.

If he could do it, so could I.

My routine also called for me to drive to Valley Hospital for radiation treatment five days a week. I quickly settled in. I would leave home at 8:00 a.m. and head to Valley for the radiation treatment that would end around 9:30 a.m., just in time to start the morning session at my pediatric office.

The office was located on the first floor of my house, an ideal setup for my situation. I would work for a couple of hours in the morning and then go upstairs and sleep for two hours and then go back down again to the office for another two hours of work. My staff made sure to schedule all my appointments in those two-hour blocks. Any emergencies were handled by one of my colleagues.

At first, I could eat, but that soon changed as my body absorbed the toxins doing their necessary work. Eventually those toxins prompted all the predicted side effects, and eating became virtually impossible.

My radiation therapy was intense, and for good reason. I insisted that it be intense, over the cautious resistance of my radiation doctor. A pathology report from Pittsburgh three weeks into the blasting of my parotid area showed that prior to surgery, the cancer had spread to within one millimeter of my carotid artery, a dangerously small margin. If the malignancy had eroded the fragile layer outside that major artery, the show would have been over. I would have died.

Once I realized that, I also learned that I had not been getting a strong enough dose of radiation. So I asked for more. I simply could not take a chance of even a single cancer cell surviving radiation and later blooming into a full cancer lesion. When the radiation oncologist supervising my treatment failed to see my point, I switched to a different, far more experienced one who did. I wanted to blast that tumor with as much force and energy as possible. And so they did. With the narrow focus and the more intense blasting, my face, neck, and upper back area was severely burned and that was still evident as I danced at Sheeraz's wedding.

The side effects were unpleasant and intensely painful. I developed horrendous sores inside my mouth, and I could eat practically nothing. With my taste buds destroyed by radiation, whatever I could force down tasted like a piece of cardboard. The focused and powerful radiation actually burned holes in my jaw and sent small fragments of bone extruding into my cheek. I would make several visits to a dentist so he could pull them out.

Fauzia, concerned about my weight and lack of nutrition, came to the rescue, as she always did. I'm not a big man, but I have always been conscious of what I ate. I'm not a health club habitué or a runner, but I would always make sure I kept moving and did not become a sedentary and overweight slug. I always took the stairs, never smoked or drank or indulged in drugs. All of that helped me, I'm sure. But my weight was dropping fast and I had no desire to eat. Fauzia began making me mango lassi, a Pakistani drink recipe of smooth yogurt flavored with mango pulp that somehow managed to appeal to me. That was delicious and easy to get down. I thought I could actually taste the mango flavor, but it was a mirage created by my brain. As a child, I loved mangoes and mango lassi. My brain remembered my favorite aroma and since my sense of smell was intact, recreated the taste from old memory.

As the intense radiation treatments continued, they burned the left side of my face severely. Skin was peeling off the side of my neck and shoulder, and I needed to dress the festering sores twice a day with special ointments and lidocaine and cover them in fishnet gauze that I wore like an ornate vest. I smiled though the process as much as I could, and the radiation department nurses, seeing my attempts at humor, would tease me. "You look like a geisha boy in your fishnet vest with the little belly sticking out," they would say. Humor was such a soothing balm.

Before the invasion of my body began, I realized that rest would be a precious commodity. I knew what it would do to me, and I knew I wanted to keep working. I would need to snatch as much sleep as I possibly could whenever possible.

I asked Sheeraz to rearrange an upstairs room in our house that had wide-open windows and a nice southern exposure that would let me soak up as much of the growing spring sunshine as possible.

"Bring up my comfortable recliner from downstairs, set up the TV and DVD player, and get me as many comedy tapes as you can find," I told him. If I was going to be miserable, at least I could laugh through it with Monty Python, George Carlin, and *Saturday Night Live.*

In many ways, suffering through cancer treatments is a state of mind. If you focus on the pain and the discomfort, you'll drop into a depression. The process is painful and uncomfortable and traumatic, like an annoying guest who won't leave. If you ignore it as much as possible, you can actually distract yourself from the daily grind. I focused on the end result and refused to live in the present with that ugly guest.

In the end, focusing on being well enough to dance at the wedding, focusing on the light at the end of the tunnel, I did not watch a single comedy tape.

Still, it was no blissful walk in the woods. The burns were painful and the mouth sores unbearable, but the worst part was the havoc visited on my stomach by the chemo. It drained me of energy. On one particularly vicious night, it got to the point where it felt as if I had an insidious demon clawing to get out of my stomach ever so slowly. So the process would be as painful and protracted and torturous as possible. Even the morphine-derivative pain pills I had would not help. Nothing helped, and the pain continued relentlessly, gnawing at me from inside and out.

Fauzia, seeing my normal shell of reserve unraveling, crawled in bed beside me and began massaging my back, gently and soothingly. Her touch was a gift, more comforting than the powerful painkillers. She kept it up all night as the pain continued, and it provided enough respite that from time to time, I actually nodded off, free for moments from the relentless and rude intrusion that had become my new normal.

It was a difficult night, but unfortunately it was not the only one. Two weeks earlier that chemo had infused enough toxin into my system that my blood count had dropped dangerously low.

"You need to skip a week and get things back up closer to normal," my oncologist told me.

"No," I said. "If I take a break, the cancer gets a break. I'm not skipping anything."

"We need to do something," he said, offering the option of an injection that would stimulate the bone marrow activity and let my blood count rise. But of course there was always a downside. The injections could also produce intense bone pain.

"That's OK," I said. "I will take the pain. But I cannot afford to take any breaks."

"Make sure you stay away from any contagious patients," he cautioned.

"Like what, chicken pox?"

"No, like cold or flu or pink eye."

I chuckled. "You have no idea what pediatricians do. Do you?"

Ironically, this combination therapy, the addition of chemo to radiation after surgery, something most experts advised against except for Dr. Schaitkin and Dr. Chin, something I fought so hard for back then, is now a widely accepted and recommended treatment for salivary duct carcinoma.

I finished the chemo treatments on June 1, 2002. Because of my insistence that the radiation dosage be amped up, I didn't get my last blast of radiation until two weeks later and just one week before the wedding, hence my somewhat sketchy appearance during the wedding weekend.

I survived, though. And I danced so happily, ever so happily into the night.

CHAPTER 11
PHYSICIAN, HEAL THYSELF

2006–2009

There is always debris after a storm, no matter its strength. My own chemo-and-radiation storm was a tsunami, and it left physical and emotional debris everywhere. The two-pronged barrage did what it was supposed to—it killed cancer cells. As expected, there was lingering damage, side effects from the massive invasion. In euphemistic military-speak, my body had become collateral damage. But the cancer had not claimed my mind, which I still needed to beat this thing.

I tired easily. I had various aches and sudden twinges of pain like I'd never had before. Total and permanent paralysis of the left half of my face, along with that of the left half of the tongue and throat, created numerous difficulties in daily life. Simple tasks like speaking, smiling, blinking, eating, chewing, and swallowing were often frustratingly difficult. No matter, I considered all that as just a small price for my life. "I must not complain about my facial paralysis," I reminded myself. After all, it was this paralysis that sounded the alarm bells that led to the discovery of the cancer. Without that, the cancer would have continued to spread undetected until it was too late. Even facial paralysis was the proverbial blessing in disguise.

So I learned to accept all that and started feeling pretty good, very good, in fact. I felt I was close to victory, and victory would be sweet. My energy level improved enough to allow a full-time work schedule.

When you're waiting for bad news, anxiety can often drive the bus. You expect the crash of that monstrous weight that had been hanging by a thin thread over your head any minute. When you are in such a state, time passes slowly, barely inching along. It is always a very tense time with that sensation of not knowing.

When things are pleasant and wonderful, you look up and years have passed. I found myself in such a state two years after Sheeraz's wedding. Two years of survival, if not perfect health, was a wondrous milestone, especially with the insidious salivary duct carcinoma at the helm, which killed most people within two years.

By the time I went to Pittsburgh to see Dr. Schaitkin for my two-year checkup, Sheeraz was married and well on his way to finishing his pediatric residency at Methodist Medical Center in Brooklyn where he continued to excel. Each month, he would send me his monthly evaluations by his teachers, full of high praise and accolades, making my heart swell with pride. One particular comment near the end of his residency said, "Dr. Iqbal has all the makings of a gifted pediatrician. I have no doubt that an excellent future awaits him." It brought tears to my eyes and a flashback to 1973 and my mentor Dr. Webber's kind words.

Noreen had graduated from NYU and was about to embark on a career at ABC Television Network, and our baby boy, Daniyal, was flourishing in high school. Fauzia, as always, stood by me unflinchingly, and we were both looking at the bright light at the end of the long tunnel. I looked back, and it seemed only a year or so prior that my three beautiful children were helpless infants. Now they were about to emerge as independent and strong adults, and the thought that I would see them go through the next phases of their lives was nothing short of miraculous.

I had shifted goals. Where initially it had been short term, to make it to Sheeraz's wedding, I later became more optimistic, but guardedly so. I stretched the next goal to three years, to when Sheeraz would join my practice. I was assured along the way by MRIs every three months of my head and neck. All came back normal. There was no sign of the return of cancer.

In summer of 2004, two years after that 2002 barrage, I saw Dr. Schaitkin for a follow-up. He was absolutely delighted by the results.

"Two years is the most difficult landmark," he told me in Pittsburgh, sitting across the same desk in the same office where thirty months before he had dropped the bomb.

He needn't have reminded me, but he added, "Most people don't make it this far."

Then he told me something I had not been aware of when my true struggle started. He had had another patient receive the same diagnosis around the same time I was slapped with mine. I assume he felt it would have been of little solace to me to have mentioned it then. "That patient died," he said gently. This is a huge landmark for you. But we cannot yet assume or guarantee that you've made it, that you are now home free. But maybe you are an exceptional case. Perhaps you are home free."

One thing I've learned and have taken to heart: one must never assume anything when dealing with something as predatory as cancer. As elated as I felt after listening to Dr. Schaitkin, I never let my guard down.

In 2006, still watchful and still cautiously wary, I began to have minor chest pains. As it turned out, they were the result of work-related stress, but when one is a cancer survivor—and that is how I viewed myself—it is always best to be watchful. Even though the chest pains disappeared within a couple of days, I decided to see my internist, who suggested I go for a CT scan of my lungs, "Just to be safe."

The CT scan revealed five tiny lesions, described medically as "small spiculated nodules"—two in my right lung and three in my left. The largest was only eight millimeters wide—about the size of a pea.

It was a small miracle that I was having those chest pains, because otherwise the continuing MRIs of my neck and throat would never have detected the new growths. It was the perfect combination of sheer good luck and my continued diligence.

I called Dr. Schaitkin immediately and flew back to Pittsburgh in March 2006 for a biopsy of the nodules. They were cancerous, and it was the same salivary duct carcinoma. My aggressive nemesis was once again slyly replicating itself from a new home base in my lungs, establishing a beachhead from which to expand.

Dr. Schaitkin, gracious and concerned as he always was, arranged for a meeting with a staff oncologist, and two days later, the three of us sat down for what was a productive and frank discussion that centered around one rather harsh point: there was no treatment for recurring salivary duct carcinoma. Few people survived the initial onslaught, and cases where it had metastasized, where it returned elsewhere in the body, were extremely resistant to all treatments. No one had ever reported a successful treatment of metastasized salivary duct carcinoma.

So what was next? There was no literature to guide us. We were flying by the seats of our pants, and none of us knew what to expect. Even grimmer was the prospect that whatever we tried, chances were it would not work. But I had made it this far and the fighter in me still had some energy left. I would continue the battle.

Despite the oncologist's frankness about my continued odds of survival, I knew what I had to do. I was blessed in a way. My luck once again emerged and settled nicely into my lap. Pathology results had revealed the presence of Her2, human epidermal growth factor receptor 2. In fact, the pathology results were "highly positive." One hundred percent of the cancer cells from my lungs exhibited Her2.

Only a few years before, scientists had discovered that certain malignant and progressive breast cancers had surface markings called Her2, which readily allowed the nutrition a cancerous cell needed to grow and thrive. In other words, the presence of Her2 on the surface of cancer cells indicates and facilitates a rapid growth of the cancer. Let's look at it in another way. If we were to think of a cancer as an important large building that has been taken over by a group of terrorists, then Her2 would be like the loading dock in that building. The terrorists in the building need some essential supplies, especially food, to survive and thrive. The trucks carrying such nutrients would need the building's loading dock to park and unload their cargo. We can see how important these loading docks, the Her2 receptors, are to the cancer cells. The higher the number of Her2 receptors, the more aggressive the cancer and the more rapidly it grows. Likewise, if we can somehow block those loading docks, we could significantly thwart the growth, even the survival, of the cancer cells.

Only recently, a drug called Herceptin had been developed that was successful in treating aggressive breast cancers that were Her2 positive. In effect, Herceptin blocked the loading dock and made it impossible to deliver the supply of nutrients. With Herceptin, you would be parking an empty truck at the dock, thus blocking the other trucks carrying nutrients.

Initially, Herceptin use was approved only for the end stage Her2-positive breast cancers. Then in 2006, just a few months before this meeting, the FDA expanded the approval for all cases of breast cancers, provided they were Her2 positive. But this approval was limited to certain types of cancers of the breast only.

That is what the three of us talked about that sunny afternoon in Pittsburgh. "Why could I not use Herceptin to treat my recurrence?" I questioned. After all, my cancer was highly positive for Her2. It was just not located in the breast.

"For one thing," the oncologists reminded me, "the literature, so far at least, has not shown any successful treatment of metastasized salivary duct carcinoma. None. As for Herceptin, only one researcher has tried it on a handful of parotid cancer patients but had no success at all."

"Perhaps, I would be the first one," I said.

Prompted by my obstinacy, the oncologist then told me there were some clinical trials underway using Herceptin in combination with some other fairly toxic new chemo drugs to treat breast cancer.

"Would you be willing to enroll in one of those trials?" he asked.

The problem with that, as far as I was concerned, was not the use of Herceptin but the other chemicals. These trials were in the very early stages, called Phase I, when physicians know very little about the side effects of the chemical cocktails. I did not want to be a guinea pig.

"Can we just use Herceptin alone?"

"No, because it has not been approved to treat salivary gland cancers."

I understood, of course, but was disappointed. As usual, I was not ready to give up. My persistence in asking questions and insisting on different perspectives had kept me alive so far. As a physician myself, I had great respect for the opinions of others and the long and deliberate processes on which those opinions were based. But I had also developed a healthy sense of skepticism by that time, testing what was held as conventional wisdom. I was living proof of that.

"I think I will wait and weigh my options," I said.

Dr. Schaitkin glanced up at me, a whisper of a smile emerging. "Of course you will," he said calmly and evenly, as if I had told him the sun would set that evening.

"I guess that's fair," the oncologist said. "You are still healthy, and things are moving slowly."

Then came a slightly ominous exchange, meant, I'm convinced, not to alarm me but to remind me.

"Is there anything you have thought about doing, any dream that you have not yet fulfilled? Now might be the time to do it."

Fauzia mentioned that we had always wanted to go for a pilgrimage to Makkah.

"By all means, do it. I think now would be the best time for it while you are still in good health."

He was politely but clearly telling me that the salivary duct carcinoma in my lungs was going to kill me. But would it do so quickly or slowly? I needed research, and I needed creative thinking and more expert opinions. No one had so far told me I would beat this. No one said I would be fine. Did I have just a little time, perhaps some time, or a bit more? Soon after as we sat in his office, Dr. Schaitkin made what I felt later was a most poignant observation.

"This is the first time I have ever seen a recurrence of this cancer four years later. This is a very aggressive cancer. It comes back within a few months, two years max. Sajjad, there must be something in your body that is fighting this cancer."

I sat there as it sank in but said nothing.

"Why did it take four years to show up again?" Dr. Schaitkin added. "Your immune system has been fighting this thing all along, and it is at least slowing it down."

I smiled briefly.

Dr. Schaitkin continued, "I don't think you have to rush into any kind of decision," he said, almost reassuring me. "Take your time and think about it. You have time. Of course, we should monitor the cancer with periodic CT scans."

I took some small comfort from that conversation, but I still had the cancer to face and decisions to make. What seemed certain was that it would eventually kill me. But I took to heart the oncologist's advice to start doing things I had dreamed of doing. One trip that had been on my "someday" list was a pilgrimage to Makkah, a H*ajj*, or in my case, a smaller version of it called Umrah.

For Muslims, nothing compares to the Hajj or Umrah. It is a spiritual journey that is actually an obligation for those who have the good health and money to make the trip— and I had both, at least for the foreseeable future. The pilgrimage, which Fauzia and I made together in May 2006, is meant to remind those who make the commitment of their faith and trust in God. It will bring about a deep spiritual transformation, the faithful believe.

I believed, and there was no better time to confirm my faith than at that time, when I was heading once again into the unknown over my health. Once again, I turned to the specialists. Once again, there were no clear answers.

I continued to have CT scans of my lungs every three months, which showed that though the nodules were growing, they were doing so slowly. This confirmed Dr. Schaitkin's assessment that I had something in my body that was slowing a cancer that normally grew explosively. So what was I to do?

I spoke with an expert at Sloan, who told me not to waste my time with Herceptin, because it wouldn't help and once again reminded me that there was no known treatment for recurrent salivary duct carcinoma.

I reached out to a good friend of my wife's, Farida, who was an oncologist in Long Island. She agreed with the need to use Herceptin and recommended the addition of a "gentler" chemotherapy drug as well. The problem was that she was too far away.

I corresponded with an expert in thoracic surgical on-cology from the University of Virginia, to whom I had sent my CT scans. Yes, he wrote back, it would be fairly easy to surgically remove all those nodules. However, there would be no point in doing so until we knew that there weren't many more cancers germinating in other parts of my lungs ready to sprout soon after surgery. "And they usually do," he said. He asked me to get in touch with him if there was no further growth over the next two years. Only then would he consider performing the operation. I could tell he did not think that was likely.

"I might not have two years," I thought.

Then came a much-needed break, though I had to ad-mit that by that time, I was making my own breaks and was ornery in my insistence about using Herceptin.

In September 2006, I went to Boston to meet with Dr. Robert Haddad, an eminent oncologist and the head and neck cancer expert at Dana Farber Cancer Institute. Dr. Haddad had conducted, until then, the only clinical trial of Herceptin against salivary gland cancers. The study in-volved a total of fourteen patients from six medical centers with various types of salivary gland cancers, all Her2 posi-tive. This small number illustrates how rare salivary gland cancers are, and the rarest of the rare are those with Her2 positivity. Thirteen of those patients did not respond to Herceptin, and only one patient had a partial response. The study had been abandoned for the lack of enough patients and a very poor response rate. That study was then cited by numerous other oncologists as proof that Herceptin was not effective against salivary gland cancers. That assump-tion was completely false.

But at least Dr. Haddad had recognized the potential for using Herceptin in my type of cancer. When we met in Boston that afternoon, I was immediately struck by his kind and calm manner. Dr. Haddad was knowledgeable, as expected, but also very thoughtful, logical, and deliberate. He was also most generous with his time, as we spent almost two hours in his office discussing my dilemma.

One thing came to light that afternoon: the vast majority of the salivary gland cancers are not Her2 positive. However the salivary duct carcinoma, the kind I had, stood out in bold contrast. Most, about 80 percent, tended to be Her2 positive.

"Shouldn't we," I questioned, "do a study of Herceptin only in patients with Her2 positive salivary duct carcinoma? We might get a higher success rate. We need to have a salivary duct carcinoma, not just any salivary gland cancer, and it has to have Her2 positivity for Herceptin to work—and I have that," I said. "If it works for similar cancers in the breast, it might work for me too."

Dr. Haddad agreed that I had a valid point.

"It does make sense. If you can find an oncologist who will agree to try Herceptin, I think you should give it a shot," he said.

I was elated. I finally had the approval and the blessing to try Herceptin—and from such an eminent expert, too! Armed with that, I could surely find a local oncologist to prescribe and administer the medicine.

As a footnote, in 2013, Robert Haddad and his associates published another study of Herceptin-based treatment in thirteen patients with my type of cancer and reported a significant success rate.

At the end of my visit, spontaneously and surprisingly, he did something that I had never expected. There was an upcoming meeting of prominent researchers of salivary gland cancers from around the world at the National Cancer Institute in Washington, DC. The meeting was not open to the public or other physicians, but he could get me an invitation, he said.

Of course I jumped at the chance. I thought it would be terrific and would allow me to see if, somewhere in the world, there was some study going on about the use of Herceptin or any other medicine—some blast of good news about trials or some small measure of success, something to indicate that someone somewhere had at least thought of it. Something encouraging, I hoped.

I very much wanted to be a fly on the wall listening.

So I sat for an entire day in October of 2006 as experts from Portugal, Israel, the United Kingdom, France, the United States, and Japan detailed their studies in earnest to curious colleagues.

I learned nothing and left dejected and disappointed. It seemed that all I heard was "Nothing seems to be working"—all a function of the cold fact that because of the rarity of the disease, there were few people to study, which in turn meant there was little grant money available.

At the end of the meeting, I cornered one of the eminent oncologists I had consulted with four years before. I was frustrated. I explained my situation and the similarities between my cancer and Her2-positive ductal carcinoma of the breast.

"Yes," she said, "I agree. Treat it the way you would treat Her2-positive breast cancer."

So I set out to find an oncologist who would be willing to prescribe Herceptin for me in the face of zero evidence supporting its efficacy. And on top of that, the oncologist would also have to be willing to administer and monitor the program of what would be a unique one-patient clinical trial.

I found the right person in my own backyard. Indu Sharma, an oncologist, was actually a colleague at Valley Hospital in Ridgewood. She would soon prove to be a godsend.

I visited with Dr. Sharma in her Mahwah office, only a few miles from my home. I explained my situation in great detail, as I had with countless other physicians before. It had become a rote speech by then. I think she began to understand clearly that I was not a typical patient—but in a good way.

Dr. Sharma was very kind, and it appeared she quickly grasped that I had used my medical knowledge, research, and analysis skills to create a plan, albeit a plan that was not based in the academic literature. Yes, my request for Herceptin was unconventional, and yes, no one seemed to have done this before for my type of cancer.

But she smiled slightly as she moved a folder on her desk and looked me directly in the eye.

"OK, I'll do it."

Those four words, after so many thousands I had expended and listened to during the latest fight, were sweet, terse, and nothing short of wonderful.

Herceptin is not a take-two-aspirin-and-call-me-in-the-morning kind of drug. It is toxic, and as such, in certain patients, it can destroy the heart or lungs and otherwise wreak havoc, causing serious and occasionally fatal infusion reactions.

Dr. Sharma designed a chemical regimen for me that called for intravenous infusion of Herceptin once a week. Because of the potential side effects, she recommended I have an echocardiogram of my heart every three months.

To establish a base and to make sure my organs could withstand the assault, she advised that I first have a battery of blood tests and an echocardiogram before I started the regimen. If my heart and lungs were already weakened, there would be no Herceptin, no attempt at this unusual program I had designed. To the delight of everyone, my heart and lungs were in great shape and the green light flashed.

I was off and running.

Three months into my Herceptin program, the cancer in my lungs was unchanged; in normal cases, it would have grown substantially. We would all have loved to see the nodules shrinking, of course, but this was still good news. I was more than holding my own, and in many ways, I was a trailblazing pioneer. We were buying time, and time is a substantial gift many cancer patients do not have, especially those with recurrent or metastatic salivary duct carcinoma.

I did have side effects over the eight months I was on the regimen. Side effects for chemo patients are as sure as the sun rising and setting. They will happen, and the only uncertainty is what they will be and their severity.

Mine included spiking malaria-like fevers with temperatures up to 105 degrees F and lows below normal. They were bad enough at one point that Dr. Sharma recommended hospitalization to investigate the cause of these fever spikes. But I chose not to go.

"It can't be anything other than the Herceptin," I said. "I would prefer to do all the testing as an outpatient if that's OK with you."

She consented. A battery of lab tests and X-ray studies all came back negative.

Herceptin treatment was discontinued, and, sure enough, my fever started to come down. Once my system fully recovered, Dr. Sharma restarted Herceptin, but on a once-every-three-weeks schedule, which I tolerated very well.

As with all treatments like this, cancer eventually begins to adapt and counter. That is what makes it so frustrating and insidious. So it was that some twenty months into treatment that the Herceptin seemed to have lost its effect as the gatekeeper of the loading dock. No one was surprised.

By January 2009, twenty-two months after I started my unconventional Herceptin regimen, CT scans of my lungs showed a substantial increase in the size and number of nodules in my lungs. The cancer had learned how to deal with Herceptin—just as I had learned by then to deal with the backslides, shocks, and bad news that come hand in hand with being a cancer patient. I had plan B in my back pocket, neatly tucked away for when it would be necessary. I knew at some point I would need it.

Maybe now it was time for surgery. I remembered my conversation with the thoracic surgeon in Virginia almost two years before who termed the cancer nodules in my lungs as "easily resectable," meaning they were easy to reach and remove. I returned to Pittsburgh, where surgeons agreed that surgery might be a worthwhile option. But of course there were problems.

Surgically removing the nodules when they were still growing and multiplying was not expedient. Why remove them when others would almost surely crop up? It was a temporary solution that would provide temporary relief at best. It was rearranging the deck chairs on the *Titanic* as the ship was sinking. It was sheer folly at worst.

It would be a major surgery lasting for several hours with significant risk of serious complications and a long and painful recovery period lasting a couple of months. My chest would be cut open and lifted up like a clamshell, or I would need two ten-inch incisions, one on each side of my chest, running from the top front all the way to the bottom back of my chest. In the back of my mind, I remembered a patient who had died from just that kind of surgery. But that was not the worst part.

The bigger dilemma, in my mind, was the very real probability of the appearance of new cancer lesions in other parts of the lungs a few months after the surgery. What would I do then? I would be left with no options. Doing the same surgery again was out of the question.

"How about VATS surgery?" I asked.

Laproscopy and laproscopic surgery have been around for a number of years. One or more small incisions are made on the belly, and the inner anatomy is visualized by inserting a thin scope fitted with a tiny video camera. The surgeon can also insert specially made instruments through the scope to perform many surgical procedures, such as tying the fallopian tubes or removing an appendix.

Only during the last decade or so had the use of a similar technique become possible in thoracic surgery. It was called VATS, for video-assisted thoracic surgery.

I was convinced that VATS was the ideal strategy to remove the cancers in my lungs. It would still be a major surgery. I would need several different incisions, several different procedures. It would take a few hours. Yet, compared with the traditional method, the recovery would be far quicker and take only a couple of weeks versus a couple of months.

Most important, VATS could be done again. With the conventional surgery, it was basically a "one and done." You couldn't go back and do it again. But I could, possibly, have VATS done again and again if the new cancer nodules appeared. This was my best option, I thought.

"Can my surgery be done as VATS?"

I was told that it couldn't be done. My entire journey had been full of "it can't be done," and it was so tiring to hear that again and again. I left after giving my usual answer, "I will think about it."

I thought if I were to have any surgery to remove the nodules, it should at least be done at a local hospital near the comforts of home. Those comforts included a true jaw-dropper, a shock that took some time to recover from. The hospital had just brought on board a new and well-qualified thoracic oncology surgeon who had been trained at Memorial Sloan Kettering. My initial reaction was that once again I had somehow been graced with good luck.

I made an appointment and sent my complete history, CT scans, copies of the biopsy reports—the full details—to his office so he could review them beforehand. The day of my appointment, after forty-five minutes of waiting, I was called in to the examination room. The doctor walked in, dropped tiredly into his chair, and leaned back.

"Who told you there were metastases in your lungs?" he asked.

"Excuse me?" I said, jolted.

"I have reviewed CT scan of your lungs. Who told you they were metastatic nodules?"

I sat upright, my head spinning. Was he trying to tell me that after all this time, all this research and discussion and treatment, that those nodules were not cancerous? It was bizarre and unsettling to say the least.

"Did you see the radiologist's report?" I sputtered.

"I have looked at your CT scan. These nodules are spiculated. I have never heard of the spiculated nodules being cancerous."

Flabbergasted, I listened as a sentence from the textbook flashed before my eyes, "A spiculated edge is an independent predictor of malignancy in a lung nodule."

"I don't think these are cancerous," he insisted.

"Did you see the biopsy reports?"

"Oh, you had a biopsy too? Where was it done? What did it show?"

"Doctor, did you view the CT scan only? Did you not look at anything else I sent you? Yes, there is a biopsy report in there from UPMC, and it showed that these nodules are cancerous."

"Well, I have my doubts," he persisted. "I have never heard of spiculated nodules being cancerous."

I was dumbfounded. I felt as if I were talking to a member of the Flat Earth Society, a Luddite denier of what years of cancer research had clearly established.

This was the new and highly regarded surgeon? This was the new head of the hospital's oncology section? How had he managed to be hired, how had he established such a good reputation or even gotten through the rigorous program at Sloan? I will never know, but fighting him was a battle I did not have the time or energy for. I was stunned.

If I had listened to him before, if our paths had crossed two years earlier, right after the nodules were first spotted, if I had put blind faith in him, I would be dead, pure and simple.

I would have been relieved at his "finding" that those growing cancerous nodules in my lungs were benign and would never have started the Herceptin, never put myself through the side effects and the waiting, the irritation and the anxiety.

I would have lived in false hope and died miserably. I would have enjoyed the brief respite from his cockeyed and incorrect diagnosis, and I would have died. Perhaps there is a lesson there, something positive from such a strange encounter.

"Let me talk to Pittsburgh. Just leave their telephone number with my nurse, and I will call them on Monday," he said.

"That's OK. You shouldn't bother," I told him, a tinge of what I can describe only as disgust in my voice.

I walked out and never returned. At this point in the game, he was either on my team or he wasn't, and after five minutes, I knew that he was not.

CHAPTER 12
A COMPROMISE

March 2009

The new thoracic surgeon's pronouncement was nothing short of appalling, and it shook me to my core. I picked my jaw up from the floor and ran for my life, literally. I did not look back.

As 2009 frigidly crept over Ridgewood and slowed the normal New Jersey frenzy to a more sedate though slush-covered pace, two things became clear. That, in turn, led to a logical conclusion. First, my Herceptin regimen had done its job and kept my cancer in check for twenty-two months. But cancer is wily and had adapted, which produced the second revelation: my dormant nodules were growing and multiplying. The conclusion, then, was that I would need surgery to remove the nodules. This revelation was neither surprising nor upsetting. At this point, I was numb to news like this. I just had to keep moving and thinking and trying whatever I possibly could to stay ahead of it.

I had been prepared for it. In fact, it was my only option. We had known that the probability was high that the cancer would return. I felt like Alice in Wonderland, like I'd fallen down the rabbit hole and woken up in an alternative universe as a survivor left to battle a voracious cancer that took no prisoners and left no survivors.

Open-chest surgery was far from gentle. It was an exhausting process with a long recovery period, one that often left patients wrapped in a blanket of depression as a result of the medical process and emotional effects. It was also a one-shot deal. So intense and destructive are these open-chest lung surgeries that as necessary and potentially life-saving as they are, surgeons will perform them only once for any patient. You just cannot go back again. I certainly didn't want to have any surgery to remove my growing lesions too early. What if there were other dormant cancer lesions waiting to sprout after surgery?

So I had waited until the last possible minute. Now it was time. I had held the enemy at bay long enough. I entered the fray on two fronts: first, I was fighting my returning cancer, and second, I was once again fighting the medical experts. This time around, it was to question surgeons who had previously rejected my suggestion that they could use the less-disruptive VATS. In the euphemism of medicine and surgery, VATS is "minimally invasive," but such terms are relative. While it is less intrusive than open-chest surgery, I would still have to face hours of various instruments being pulled in and out of my lungs. It was no walk in the park.

Knowing I would eventually face surgery, I began querying surgeons around the country who specialized in chest-cancer surgery about using a VATS procedure to excise my growing number of lesions. I visited one in Pittsburgh and one in Boston, and I spoke to a third in Virginia. "Why can't you take the more polite video path?" I asked.

It can't be done, they said, uniformly and emphatically. It has to be an open-chest procedure. Their reason made sense. A CT scan might miss smaller lesions, smaller than a grain of rice. But an experienced surgeon can often detect those by rolling his or her fingers along the smooth surface of the lung. If the surgeon detects any such tiny "pebble," he or she can remove that too and nip it in the bud. "You simply can't do that through a scope," they said. It made sense.

My objection also made sense, and it was simple. The open-chest procedure would require a minimum of two months of recovery time—and with it came a significant amount of potential complications. The clincher for me was very clear: since I had an aggressive cancer that was very likely to return, why not try the VATS, which had a faster recovery time and fewer complications? Most important, it could be done again if cancer came back. I could have more than one procedure—though God knows I hoped I wouldn't need to.

"We can't," they said again. We need to go in and actually touch and feel the entire surface of both lungs to test for the telltale hardness. If they seem unusual, we can remove them. We can't do that with a camera."

I knew if I agreed to an open-chest procedure and six months or a year later the cancer returned, my fight would be over. They couldn't go in again, and I'd be facing the inevitable result—a slow and ultimately painful passing, my chest now closed permanently. The gate would close, and the cancer would have free rein.

This is not how my story would end.

Their concerns were valid, but so were mine. I was again at odds with the medical establishment.

I needed to find someone who would agree to VATS, someone I could convince that I needed an option that dealt specifically with my unusual and voracious cancer. If it came back, I wanted to have a chest and lungs that would be in good enough shape to do it all again. VATS was the only option for that.

As luck would have it, I found one of the country's most experienced VATS surgeons not too far from home, in the woodsy and tony South Jersey suburbs about an hour-and-a-half drive from Ridgewood.

Dr. Jeanne Phillippe Bocage and his associates had done more than 1,500 VATS procedures when I found him. He was the second most acclaimed VATS surgeon in the country.

When I visited him at his New Jersey office, I told him of my dilemma, headlined by my accounts of the various surgeons who said they had to feel for the signs of cancerous nodules on the lung's surface, not merely look at them through a camera.

I can still vividly place myself in that moment; I can still picture Dr. Bocage as he sat quietly mulling over my unusual request. The scene comes back to me so clearly for two reasons: Dr. Bocage's smile when he began speaking and the fact that he agreed to something so exceptional and unheard of to that point.

"We can compromise," he said.

I was happily stunned.

He explained that normally surgeons using VATS would make four one-inch incisions on both sides of the chest into which they can insert both the camera probe and the necessary instruments.

"An inch is just enough room for the instruments," he said, "and that is why the other surgeons are correct about feeling. With only an inch of room, there is no way I could get inside with my hands."

I had always understood that.

"But it is not written in the Bible that the incisions have to be only one inch. Why can't I do two-inch incisions? That will allow me to fit a finger or two into your chest cavity, and I can feel every part of your lung."

I smiled, relieved. What an ingenious, yet incredibly simple solution!

"I'm confident this will work," he added.

Then came the caveat. It might not have been written in the Bible that one-inch incisions are sacrosanct, but one must always understand that somewhere in the Book of Life, it is written in large boldface type that "There is always a caveat."

I was relieved to hear Dr. Bocage's pronouncement; it seemed a minor one. If for any reason he found a potentially cancerous lesion he could not reach with his VATS instruments, I must consent to his switching gears and performing open-chest surgery to remove it.

There would be no other option, of course. He couldn't simply leave it behind and say, "I could not get it."

Since I would be anesthetized in the event that happened, I had to sign a consent form beforehand.

"How often does this happen?" I asked.

"In about 1 percent of the cases, but we have to cover all the bases."

I agreed quickly. There was one further negotiation. Such surgeries are normally done on one lung at a time, which of course in nearly all cases makes sense. If there are serious complications, such as a collapsed lung or one that has to be removed completely, the patient still has one good lung. However, I did not want to have to go through this procedure twice and pleaded to have both of my lungs operated on at the same time.

"I'll take my chances," I said. "I have full faith in you."

"You will suffer from a lot of pain on both sides of the chest, rather than just one side. Recovery will be very difficult on you," he warned.

"I will handle the pain. I have had worse."

He agreed reluctantly.

My loving family had by that time grown to accept my occasional hospital visits and had actually developed a familiar routine. Sheeraz rented a suite at a hotel near the Somerset Medical Center and we *all* settled in to a relaxed and hopeful pre-surgery evening in which we actually enjoyed ourselves and joked, lightheartedly covering whatever tension might have been present. By then, we had all grown used to these interruptions.

Despite the mental image formed by visions of tiny instruments being inserted precisely into small incisions, there was nothing dainty about my surgery. By the time Dr. Bocage finished the five-hour operation on March 9, 2009, at Somerset Medical Center, he had removed about 20 percent of my lung tissue. He was pleased, he told me when I awoke. With only one tiny exception, he said he had gotten everything. The tiny exception would return later, but he told me there was no way to deal with it at the time.

I knew Dr. Bocage was a skillful surgeon. He was able to remove the visible lesions plus three others he felt were suspicious. I could not have asked for anything more. I was ready to go home immediately. My post-surgery stay was as expected—only three days—which was remarkably short.

The morning I rose to get out of there and head home, things had been moving along at a pleasant pace until I shed my hospital gown and tried to slip on some comfortable pajama bottoms. I could not pull them up over the distended belly that had expanded unnoticed while I lay in bed. Surprised, shocked actually, I went home wearing my hospital gown. I had been so happy with the results of the surgery and so intent on how my chest felt, I had not even noticed that my belly had expanded so much.

I had been having post-surgery stomach pains but had written them off as by-products of the narcotic painkillers I'd been getting. Over the next few days, as I sat at home, I continued to have severe chest pains. The incisions on both sides of my chest made it difficult to lie on either side and get any sort of decent sleep. That was expected.

I had not expected the stomach pains, though, and neither had the doctors. My stomach distension continued. An endoscopy a month later showed that my stomach was paralyzed—truly not working at all—a likely complication from the lung surgery. All it would take would be a slight tug or a misplaced pull on a nerve while surgeons were attending to the main show to set off this paralysis. Doctors felt my stomach would improve on its own in due course—and it did with some medication and patience. But even today it has not returned to normal and I still exercise caution when eating—no big meals, which I would suppose is not an entirely bad thing.

Fauzia and I had developed another routine during this war with my cancer. We used major medical events as a benchmark, a minor hurdle, to signal it was time to focus on some sort of enjoyable reward. I'd used Sheeraz's wedding to get through the chemo and radiation barrage. Now we set another goal. After my chest surgery, Fauzia and I set our sights on a nice and relaxing European vacation. That would be our enticement to get through the recovery process from surgery. It is nice to have something to look forward to after the misery—something alluring to pull you through the tougher times.

In June 2009, two months after Dr. Bocage worked his magic, we left for what proved to be a wonderful trip to Paris, Amsterdam, and Venice for two weeks of leisurely travel. Our minds and eyes turned to the Louvre, the wonders of Dutch hospitality, and the Grand Canal instead of chest pains and CT scans. We both couldn't wait to leave that all behind.

We returned to yet another of the predictable undulations every cancer patient must face. With cancer, there is never a point at which you arrive and are told, "You're home free now; you are completely and totally and irrevocably cured." Certainly, and I know this very well, there is a point where you feel comfortable that you're in a good and safe position. I'm there now, in fact. But one must reconcile to always living with the presence of doubt—not fear, but only an occasional flash of justified concern. It is not unpleasant or negative or even disruptive; it is just there and a presence one must acknowledge. It was like a secret others had guessed but never talked about publicly.

In those undulations, the ups are invigorating and the downs suffocating if you allow them to be. You must move one simple step forward at a time, live in one single moment at a time. That is a cancer patient's sacred obligation. You savor every glowing, exciting positive burst. Doing anything less is unacceptable.

In our first post-surgery meeting, Dr. Bocage told me he was quite pleased with the results. He felt he had gotten everything—with that one possible exception. He had seen a nodule through his lens that he could not reach to feel and, if necessary, remove. It had not appeared on the CT scans from the previous two years.

"We don't know if it is cancerous or not. That is my only concern about the entire procedure."

Then he handed me an eight-by-ten-inch glossy photograph of the suspicious nodule—a sort of parting gift that I could stare right in the face. At last, the potential enemy was in plain sight.

"Why didn't you try to reach it?" I asked as I stared at the picture. The little fingernail-sized, dark-pink, fleshy lump sitting way back in the center of the photograph looked pretty nondescript, yet could have such grave consequences. Why was it left behind? It seemed that the tiny intruder sat in a position that would require removing my entire lung to get at it. It was not unlike having a small speck at the base of a stem holding an apple to a tree. To get to it, you'd have to lop off the apple.

"At this point, we don't even know if it is cancerous," Dr. Bocage said. "It would be catastrophic to go after it, remove your entire lung, and then find out it was benign—a very serious mistake and certainly not worth it."

"I assume you couldn't take a biopsy from it?"

"I tried, but it was too far away and couldn't be reached with a biopsy needle. Let's just monitor it closely and see if it grows."

I was concerned. My slate was not quite as clean as I had expected. But it was certainly eminently cleaner than it had been. Post-surgery biopsies had revealed that each nodule Dr. Bocage had painstakingly removed from my lungs showed the presence of salivary duct carcinoma. It was further evidence that the enemy was real and I had to continue to conquer it.

A week after that meeting and Dr. Bocage's announcement of the potentially troubling lesion, I was back in the radiology department at my local hospital with a simple question. They had been doing my CT scans for three years by then, all the way through my Herceptin regimen. Dr. Bocage's lesion had never shown in any of these scans.

"So how do we follow this?" I asked the radiologist. "How do we track this potentially cancerous nodule when it doesn't even show up now?"

His answer was simple and apparent. "If it grows big enough, we'll begin to see it."

This was not acceptable to me. I showed him the picture. The nodule was large enough even now to show up on CT scan. Why did it not?

"Isn't there anything you can do to enhance the scan—to somehow be able to get a better view of this?"

"No."

It was a predictable enough answer but one that by this time did nothing to deter me. I started my usual round of phone calls, looking for someone who could address this newcomer to the party.

My own computer searches revealed a possible answer. The latest models of CT scanners, sixty-four-slice scanners, had a much higher picture quality and could, possibly, visualize some obscure lesions not picked up by the older sixteen-slice scanners. I called the hospital and, sure enough, all my scans were done on the older CT scanners. Strangely enough, they did have a sixty-four-slice scanner, yet the radiologist never offered that option to me during our last meeting.

Once again, I found the solution close to home, at the Hackensack University Medical Center, which was able to use enhanced techniques in a scan that found Dr. Bocage's elusive lesion, which the other scans had missed.

"Now, we can track it," they told me.

In the meantime, Dr. Sharma was not prepared to sit back and wait or track anything. She wanted action. Taking a cautious path I agreed with, she told me that until it was proved otherwise, we should consider this newly revealed nodule cancerous. Using the pathology specimens from my surgery, she had the cancer analyzed further and, based upon those results, recommended a course of treatment.

Once again, I was back on chemotherapy, this time on Erbitux intravenously. Dr. Sharma warned me that it had toxic side effects on skin.

"Skin?" I almost laughed. "Who cares?" I thought after what I had been through before, skin rashes or itchy patches of dry skin were something I could deal with simply enough. I was very wrong about that, though. I learned quickly how important one's skin is.

Over the eight months I was on Erbitux, I was covered in a rash so irritating and so uncomfortable I was slathering on great dollops of lotion several times a day with only a marginal relief. My fingernails and toenails became inflamed to the point where I could not wear shoes, and I walked around in sandals, even in midwinter. There were painful open wounds on my fingers and toes that refused to heal no matter what I tried. Some tiny blood vessels on my arms would, suddenly and without any injury, open up and start oozing blood. It looked like a scene from a horror movie.

My left ear was painful and draining constantly because Erbitux had created an open sore in the middle ear cavity. I lost all hearing in the left ear. I persevered, though, as uncomfortable as that was. I had no choice.

Over the course of those eight months, one update was slowly emerging: my lesion was not changing, and this was wonderful news. During an afternoon visit with my Hackensack radiologist, Dr. Miller, as we reviewed the latest scan, he turned to me and said, "You know, this lesion looks the same as it was almost a year ago. Is it because of the Erbitux or because it was never cancerous to begin with?"

Interesting question.

I went home and gathered all my scans from the last three years, including the ones from the local hospital. The next day, I returned to Dr. Miller's office, where he started to closely examine the older scans.

Maybe it was the benefit of hindsight, of knowing where the lesion was, or perhaps more diligent and careful analysis, but he found it on all of them, even on the older scans, dating all the way back to 2006.

"It's exactly the same. It has not changed one iota. It is not cancerous."

What a relief! It was time to stop the Erbitux and bid my annoying rash a fond and appropriate good-bye.

CHAPTER 13
A NEW FIGHT, A NEW HOPE

2012

Side effects are an expected but necessary part of surviving cancer. The surgeries, drugs, and radiation do what they are designed to do—kill growing cancer cells. So it is not entirely unrealistic to expect that while they do their lethal job, some other not-so-palatable things will come along for the ride.

Add to the mix the drugs you'll get to counter those side effects and you will soon be hosting a cornucopia of chemicals your body was never designed to accommodate.

I certainly experienced plenty of side effects, everything from minor aches to skin rashes to my crumbling jawbone, the high fevers and mouth sores, and, of course, constant problems with my stomach, such as severe pains, diarrhea, vomiting, and dehydration. You could throw in loss of appetite, loss of hair, many different infections, loss of hearing in my left ear, frequent pains in the muscles and joints, and anemia, to mention a few others. Add to all that frequent hospitalizations and so many surgeries, major and minor. I also had to deal with the stress of the warnings of potential side effects, as if a cancer patient doesn't have enough things to worry about. Herceptin might have damaged my heart or lungs if they had been weaker.

Here is the kicker, though. From my perspective, I'm happy to have endured each one of those pernicious side effects. Having them illustrated that things were working, and they were a small price to pay for life and survival.

There was also an unintended side effect I developed over the course of my treatments, and I was especially grateful for it. Every cancer patient—no matter what stage he or she might be in—faces the disquieting and rarely talked about fear hovering in the background, the constant awareness of what is going on in your body, of waiting for the other shoe to drop. It was not unlike sleeping with one eye open, fearing for the next sign my unwanted guest was about to drop in again. If my cancer was going to kill me, it would not do so unexpectedly, quietly, like a thief in the night. The positive side effect I actually welcomed was that I was ever vigilant and always mindful and watching for it. The one immutable truth about fighting cancer is that early detection is vital, extremely so. My continuous vigilance was a side effect of all I had been through. And it paid very nice dividends for a small investment in pain and irritation. But I never was much of a complainer. I learned early that focusing my attention on eventual survival and away from the side effects made all that pain and suffering just a little more tolerable.

Survival was the only side effect I welcomed with open arms.

A cancer survivor is never completely at rest, and neither are those closest to him or her. A sore throat that persists a day or two longer than it should sends out a warning. A sore back or a persistent cough that many people would simply write off as the flu is an alarm—or it should be. I certainly paid attention to these things. I was not inclined to be caught off guard.

And this hyper-alertness does not—or should not—fade over time. A cancer survivor is never lulled into complacency by months of good health because he or she never reaches the point where he or she thinks that cancer is permanently cured. A false sense of security is a cancer patient's worst enemy. Time and early diagnosis are the key to life and survival—the comfort and ability to continue to live well.

Don't get me wrong, this hyper-vigilance did not diminish my enjoyment of life. There is a huge difference between staying alert and being consumed by fear. I never lived in a state of constant anxiety or pessimism. I have been, and continue to be, on my guard yet always optimistic that I will fight off anything cancer can bring on.

I traveled, visited with friends, invited them to my home, and even continued to see occasional pediatric patients when Sheeraz needed my opinion. I thoroughly enjoyed the times when cancer was in remission. I loved my months free of chemo treatments and pain and dysfunctional living. I relished the opportunity to have a schedule that did not include daily or weekly medical appointments. I had wonderful vacations with Fauzia, went to baseball games with my son Sheeraz and my grandson Deen, and reveled in moments of pure bliss and the beauty of my life and my wife, children, and work.

But not a day passed when thoughts of the cancer returning were not with me like an albatross.

Even with all that, sometimes luck is the most important player in the game. If I had not had those insignificant chest pains, I never would have had the CT scans of my lungs that showed my cancer had returned. I had always managed, sometimes with a bit of luck, to stay ahead of the curve. I've been lucky that I have managed to find these ugly surprises before they got out of control.

After Dr. Bocage's deft surgery and our relaxing European trip, I was feeling good, very good in fact.

I continued to have CT scans of my lungs, and each time, they showed the cancer had not returned. In fact, even as I write this—seven years after Dr. Bocage's surgery—my lungs have been cancer free. I did not need a second lung procedure as the doctors had feared.

As always, there was a complication. It was nothing serious in my mind, more of an irritation with which I felt I could deal.

In early February 2012, I began to notice I was having an increasingly difficult time talking. At first, I felt it was likely laryngitis—it certainly sounded and felt like it. My voice was raspy, and I had trouble raising its volume and being heard clearly. At times, I was incapable of anything more than a whisper. It became an annoyance, certainly, when trying to have a conversation with someone across a room. It persisted longer than a bout of laryngitis should under normal circumstances.

My warning light came on: vigilance.

I put it aside but only temporarily. I knew I had to do something fairly soon but not just then. Fauzia and I had other plans. We had invited the entire family—the whole Iqbal clan, kids, spouses, and grandkids—for what turned out to be an absolutely spectacular Caribbean cruise. March in New Jersey is a monochromatic gray. Winter storms and the residual snow still lingered, the temperatures remained chilly, and the precipitation turned to a mix of snow, sleet, and frozen rain sometimes simultaneously. A warning about March in New Jersey should read: "Get out if you can." It is not a time for tourist posters and warm welcomes. It's plain ugly, in fact, like much of the Northeast. The allure of crisp winter snowfalls and clear biting air has long passed. We were tiring of winter, and spring was yet to blossom.

Fauzia and I realized that the perfect antidote was a blast of blue water and comforting warmth and sea breezes. The cruise was nothing short of wonderful, a true family trip I doubt anyone will ever forget. We had three adjoining cabins, suites actually, with a shared balcony on an upper deck of the beautiful ship *Liberty of the Seas,* and we sailed into the sunshine from Miami to Cozumel, where we swam with dolphins. We stopped in the Bahamas, and we ate well and relaxed the entire time. It was a perfect trip, with everyone happily mingling on their own schedules, no plans or appointments or worries in sight. In fact, as we prepared to dock back in Miami, I asked the gathered clan who had the most fun. Everyone's hand shot up.

As we headed to customs and immigration in Miami, I somehow became separated from everyone else, lagging about twenty feet behind Fauzia, who had our passports and travel documents. It was only twenty feet, a few arms' lengths. I needed to call out to Fauzia to ask her to wait for me. I tried. But nothing happened.

Not a sound came out, and I panicked. I finally caught up, and at that point, I decided something had to be done as soon as I got back to New Jersey, concerned that perhaps for the first time maybe I had waited too long to put my early-warning mantra into place.

When I got home, I called Dr. Schaitkin immediately, and we arranged for another visit to Pittsburgh, this time to the medical center's Voice and Swallowing Disorders Center.

An examination of my throat and larynx—my voice box—found that my left vocal cord was not only paralyzed but also shrinking gradually, getting atrophied. If that continued, I wouldn't be able to talk at all.

The left and right vocal cords produce sound by moving to the center of the larynx and touching each other, causing the vibrations that create sound. In normal cases, the cords move rhythmically back and forth, and we can talk and sing or otherwise make great joyful noise. My right cord was fine and moving, but since the left was paralyzed and remained stationary, there was no touching and thus no vibration and no sound, joyful or otherwise. My left vocal cord was essentially just sitting there doing nothing but shrinking away from lack of use.

That was actually the least of my problems.

"No one has ever died from not being able to talk," the doctor told me. "But people do die from aspirating food into their lungs."

My left vocal cord was not the only thing that was not functioning. The entire left side of my mouth, tongue, and throat were paralyzed too. That was what concerned the doctors most, because I would at some point have difficulty swallowing, and that could lead to choking and even suffocation—as they used to say when I was a child, having the food travel "down the wrong pipe."

Doctors, in fact, were astonished that I had not had any problems so far. I had been aware of this difficulty for the last several years and understood it for what it was, an undesirable result of my face paralysis from cancer plus surgical procedures and very aggressive radiation treatments. I had done what people have always done with a constant handicap—I adapted.

I learned to keep the food on the right side of my throat, the healthy side, and avoided the foods that were gummy or sticky and might get stuck to the left side of my tongue or cheek—foods like the dry, flaky oyster crackers I loved to nibble or another favorite, KFC biscuits, which I learned the hard way don't go down so easily when only one side of my tongue, mouth, and throat worked. I had made other concessions too. Because I could not open my mouth wide as a result of cancer surgery, I learned to use a knife and fork to eat a sandwich or a burger.

Of course, those changes and concessions had become so normal for me that I maintained to the doctors that I could eat anything I wanted.

One of the experts asked, "What foods are you able to eat?"

"I eat everything," I said.

"You can't possibly eat everything," he said.

He reached into a cupboard and brought out some saltines.

"Eat this," he said.

"Well, this I cannot eat," I said, confessing that I had problems with those KFC biscuits as well.

He laughed.

He knew I had made adjustments and had removed a number of things from my choices. I admitted also that I had problems with things that would lump together. I could take a small bite of meat, for example, chew it, and swallow it all on my right side. But something as innocuous as a spoonful of rice might accidentally slip over to the left side and cause gagging.

He suggested I have a few "swallowing therapy" sessions, and I did concede to try them when I got home, which I did for six weeks without any discernable benefit. While all this was going on, my voice continued to deteriorate. I felt that was the bigger problem.

By late April 2012, I could barely whisper.

I once again headed across the Hudson to NYU Medical Center and spoke with Dr. Milan Amin, who confirmed Pittsburgh's diagnosis. His solution, at least one that would avoid surgery, was an injection that would thicken my paralyzed vocal cord—the idea being that if it could not move into the center of my larynx to meet its moving right partner, it would expand enough to have them make contact.

The injection worked, but only passably so. I still had a fairly significant problem talking and being understood. I could produce just enough volume to be heard, but people would have to move in to understand me. There were times when I felt like Marlon Brando as Vito Corleone in *The Godfather*, with various people's ears next to my mouth. Besides, I would need these injections every three months. The process didn't seem worth it to me, given the mediocre results.

There was a surgical option that called for relocating the paralyzed vocal cord into the middle of the larynx, positioning it so the right cord would hit it rhythmically and regularly. Before the surgery could be done, however, doctors needed to know that I was cancer-free. It was major surgery after all. I understood. The pall of cancer is never far from anything. In early August 2012, I had scans of my chest, abdomen, bones, and pelvic area. They all came back negative. Relief ruled once again.

The October 2012 surgery in NYU Langone Medical Center was successful. I got my voice back, though even today, I cannot raise it to the levels I once had. All seemed well. But shortly after the surgery, the relief, and my enjoyment at speaking again, the vigilance part of the equation called for attention once again.

After coming home from the surgery, I began feeling unusual pains in my back. At first, I thought it was from sleeping in the always-uncomfortable hospital beds after surgery. I have never liked hospital beds, and this one was no different, lumpy and hard. As much time as I had spent in hospital beds, one would think I would have adapted, but this was one thing I never managed or even tried to adapt to. My solution was not to adapt but rather to get home as quickly as I could.

Vigilance.

As the back pains continued, I went to a chiropractor and told him he had two weeks to straighten things out. The pain continued, though, and by two weeks, I realized the pain had nothing to do with hospital beds. It was time for a bone scan.

The bone scan showed just what I had feared. My cancer had returned. Such is life. Less than three months after my thorough August scans revealed I was cancer free, it was back, this time in my bones. Cancer is opportunistic, and I was once again in familiar but never comfortable territory. It was time to roll up my sleeves—I was back in battle.

So I found myself in the emptying Hackensack parking lot, again facing another onslaught of cancer after so many tiring onslaughts. While I certainly was not buoyed by the news and did feel sad and disappointed, I was not panicked about it either. I was a veteran. I knew what to expect, and I knew that I would deal with it, as I had before, one day at a time, one treatment at a time.

And while my family was distraught, upset, and agitated, I returned home accepting that the remission I had hoped was permanent had merely been a temporary truce. I had been fighting for ten years by then and was seasoned, hardened, and unbowed. I would keep fighting.

I was still in love with life and quietly confident.

So while my family paced nervously and uncomfortably at the news, I went home, watched TV, and went up to bed to sleep the comforting sleep of someone not yet ready to throw in the towel.

CHAPTER 14
GLIMMERS

2012 to Present

T hough I was calm and tranquil, watched television, and slept well, the night I returned home with the news that the cancer had returned, I was not running away or trying to escape anything.

I'd learned early in the fight not to run from bad news. That did nothing but offer a head-in-the-sand moment or two of relief. The cancer was not going to disappear magically.

I can't remember what show I watched or whether I enjoyed it or not. I was already thinking about the next round and what I'd have to do. I knew more research was on the horizon, for sure. I knew information was my greatest investment—that the more I understood about what was happening, the better I could help Dr. Sharma plan my treatment.

What I didn't know that night as I drifted peacefully off to sleep was that a chance dinner-party conversation would send me down a path that would provide me with a much greater understanding of cancer treatment today and a heavy dose of the best medicine available to any cancer patient—hope.

Sparked by that dinner conversation, I would acquire through more research the knowledge that medicine was on the threshold of a new and hopeful way of treating cancer. I'd learn that I could be very close to the cutting edge. Even fifteen or twenty years ago, cancer treatment was not unlike the Dark Ages, where doctors used a one-size-fits-all approach.

I would learn that today the way medical professionals view cancer had changed so radically that it was not necessarily the almost-certain death sentence it had been. Today advancements and innovations have catapulted us into a new era of medicine where exciting new discoveries are being made on a daily basis. The wonders of the information age have allowed everyone an open access to knowledge about new drugs and technologies. I know all that now because I jumped with both feet into the fray, all because a molecular biologist serendipitously asked me a few questions and showed me that others on the forefront of cancer treatment were thinking outside the box. And that was good news, not only for me, but for anyone who had been sentenced with a cancer diagnosis.

Yes, I was back in the battle again, but I'd soon have a much stronger and greater cache of weapons to fight with. Like any cancer battle, though, there were disruptions and pains and irritations and inconveniences. These remain certain.

Another certainty in cancer treatment is a double-edged sword that provides both some small comforts packaged tidily with a bit of disconcertment. The night I learned my cancer was back, I knew that I was not alone—that I had not somehow been singled out to go through the struggle by myself. That was comforting in a way. The second thing I knew was that because there were other cancer patients to treat, Dr. Sharma was busy. The Thursday night I received the disconcerting news, she told me she'd do a literature search over the weekend and that we could sit down to talk about our options the following Tuesday. I understood. But what if she could not find enough time away from her busy life? Even if she did, two heads are better than one. I might find something she could not, or vice versa. I was not about to wait around for five days. I started my research the very next morning, sifting through the vast medical literature, searching for any report of a successful treatment of a patient like me. That was what I had always done.

I learned that there had been four case reports—only four patients just like me, who were successfully treated using Herceptin along with other drugs. Two were in Japan, one was in Los Angeles, and the fourth was in Spain. Four patients all in different parts of the world and each had salivary duct carcinoma that was Her2 positive, like me. By then, the medical community was slowly coming around to realizing the potential benefit of Herceptin in Her2-positive salivary gland cancers. It was a vindication of my insistence back in 2006 that this cancer should be treated with Herceptin even though very few experts agreed with me.

I had no time for vindications, though, and even less for I-told-you-sos. I needed an answer to my current problem. Each of the four other successful cases had used different secondary drugs, but the common thread was Herceptin, which was used as what is called a "targeted treatment," that is, against a specific vulnerability of a specific cancer—and that type only. It is a personalized treatment, not a general one.

The second drug used with Herceptin was cytotoxic, literally meaning, "poison to the cells." Such drugs kill all rapidly multiplying cells without making the good-or-bad distinction—the theory being that since cancer cells multiply rapidly, they would get killed earlier and more readily than the normal cells. Cytotoxic drugs will kill cancer cells but will also do serious damage to many normal cells—a not-so-welcome side effect. They are like a weed killer you might apply to your lawn. If you mistakenly spray it over the entire lawn rather than just the troublesome weeds, it will kill everything—the weeds, yes, and also the grass. They are indiscriminate killers.

An ideal targeted therapy will look just for the weeds—your specific cancer—and spare the grass. Herceptin targets Her2-positive cells. As mentioned earlier, Her2s are receptors on the surface of some cancer cells that play a crucial role in the growth of the cancer. Herceptin blocks Her2 and thus weakens the cancer.

The idea is this: I could use the Herceptin to weaken the cancer cells, while simultaneously using a killer cytotoxic drug to attack the weakened cancer. The beauty of targeted therapies—if you can call any infusion of chemicals into your body beautiful—is that they usually do not cause the kind of side effects so common with the conventional chemotherapy. There is usually no hair loss, severe vomiting and diarrhea, sterility, or life-threatening drops in the blood counts that come along with cytotoxins. That is not to say that using targeted therapies is like the proverbial walk in the park. There is always a potential for very serious side effects. But, in general, these medicines are easier on the patient.

As I looked at the results of those four successful treatments, I saw that the crucial component was Herceptin. The choice of the cytotoxic drug did not seem to matter much. So, I could pick a slightly better-tolerated drug to pair with Herceptin and still hope for a similar effectiveness.

For me, that was enough information to get back in the fight again.

When Dr. Sharma and I met the following Tuesday, I presented her with the printouts of those four case reports I had studied over the weekend. She reviewed them. We discussed our options, and together, we came up with a battle plan for the next round.

First, I would get a monthly injection of Xgeva, which would strengthen my frail bones—give them a bit of a push-back against the cancer that was trying hard to eat them away.

Then, I'd be back in the reclining chemo chair in her office, starting in early December 2012, receiving an hour-and-a-half intravenous infusion of Herceptin every three weeks.

For the cytotoxic component of this regimen, we picked a relatively new drug, Xeloda.

As often, there were complications. As always, my timing could not have been more fortuitous. Because I had been having quite a bit of pain in my back, I decided to have my latest scans reviewed by a radiation oncologist, Dr. Loren

Godfrey, at Hackensack University Medical Center. It was the day before Thanksgiving.

Could a radiation treatment help me? What he saw alarmed him. The cancerous lesion in my third lumbar vertebra was so large and its erosion so extensive, my spinal column was in danger of collapsing—and that would have been a serious situation permanently affecting my quality of life. Cancer had eaten away most of the bone in that vertebra, leaving behind just a weak shell that could collapse easily.

"We have no time," he told me. "This has to be addressed, and we cannot wait for the chemo to take effect. We have to do something now."

So we did. He felt so strongly about the need to act immediately he called in his staff on Thanksgiving Day to begin preparations for my treatment the next day. Friday, we began a ten-day program of zapping the vertebral lesions with high doses of radiation.

Again, I was lucky. It worked. I had made the right decision at the right time, and despite the short-term stomach problems that came with such intense and concentrated doses of radiation, it worked. I was lucky.

After the treatment, the cancer in my spine fell back into the "manageable" category. The radiation plus the Xgeva held things in control until the Herceptin could begin its work. The Xgeva made my bones thicker and harder for the cancer cells to penetrate, and the radiation shrank one of my most dangerous tumor lesions by 50 percent.

The combination was a terrific stop-gap measure. My chemo regimen also included the cytotoxic drug Dr. Sharma and I had chosen, Xeloda. I began taking it in capsule form rather than intravenously—two pills in the morning and three each night. Despite the inclination to believe that the oral form of chemo, the pills, must be gentler than the intravenous chemo, I can assure that is not so. There were troublesome side effects, but as always, I simply put up with them as best as I could, without complaining. This remained difficult at times, believe me.

Xeloda is far from benign, and with it came some of the most intense and painful stomach problems I had experienced during my entire fight. There were frequent, almost constant sores in my mouth. Even when there were no discernible sores, the lining of my mouth was sufficiently inflamed to cause burning pain if there was even a hint of spice in the food.

I had been raised on and loved Pakistani food all my life, so this created a bit of a dilemma. I could not tolerate any food that was spicy but abhorred the taste of food that was not.

Skin side effects were a big problem again. This time, it was the extreme dryness and heightened sensitivity of the skin. The bottoms of my feet were constantly inflamed, enough to cause pain on walking. Inflammation of my scalp made me lose most of my hair. But the most troubling side effects were in my stomach and intestines. Loss of appetite, a strong aversion to food, constant low-grade nausea, and stomachaches became the new norm of my life. My stomach issues persisted. Intestinal cramps became stronger and stronger. Then came the repeated bouts of a condition called paralytic ileus. This is when the intestines go on strike, are paralyzed, and stop working for a few days. There would be a complete shutdown of my bowels with excruciating pains and occasional bouts of vomiting. In fact, I found myself welcoming the vomiting because it would ease the pain, at least for a little while.

Often, I would end up in the local emergency room. They would give me intravenous fluids to correct dehydration and strong injections to relieve the pain and nausea. Once I even had to be admitted and treated as an inpatient.

The condition was temporary and self-limiting. So I started to learn to live through it for a couple of days, to accept the constant pain and vomiting and not do anything to aggravate it, such as taking anything by mouth, not even a pill. That usually worked, and my stomach would calm down after twenty-four to forty-eight hours of pure hell. Still, there were other times when I had no choice but to go to the hospital.

Eventually, I got so fed up with the frequent trips to the ER that I decided to set up an ER in my bedroom. I obtained bags of IV fluids along with all the necessary needles, tubing, and so on. I also stockpiled injections of the drugs for pain and for nausea. I injected those medicines myself. But Sheeraz or Reem, my daughter-in-law who is also a physician, would have to come in to start the intravenous infusion and monitor me. This system worked out well and kept me on Xeloda and out of the ER.

While this side drama was going on, another more positive thing was occurring. The program Dr. Sharma and I had come up with was working.

The cancer began to stabilize.

My first bone scan after three months of our new regimen—this was March 2013—showed that the cancer had spread, with several new cancer spots, but it was assumed that spread had probably occurred before we started the new treatment and before it had had enough time to take effect. Around that time, my bone pains almost completely disappeared, another sign that the treatment was working.

In June, six months later, scans showed that everything had stabilized—there were no new spots. Of course, this was good news.

I continued the regimen for almost two years but knew from experience that the devious cancer would eventually find a way to get around the defense we had set up. That is what cancer does. Herceptin had lost it effectiveness after twenty months the first time I had used it in 2007, and eventually it would do the same again. I knew that.

I knew I needed to be on high alert if and when that happened.

In the spring of 2014, satisfied with my current drug regimen and its positive effects but waiting for the inevitable, I went to a dinner party at a good friend's house in Princeton. There were maybe thirty of us there, from a large circle of friends and acquaintances, and many of us were doctors. Of course, the talk turned to medicine, sparked by recent articles on the controversy surrounding the PSA test for prostate cancer. Not your typical dinner conversation, of course, but what can you expect from doctors? Maybe it had something to do with the fact that a lot of us were middle-aged men.

Somehow the conversation meandered to breast cancer and the type that is Her2 positive.

Naturally, I had something to say about that, and I began telling them how my cancer, even though not in the breast, was Her2 positive and how I had convinced my doctors in

2007 to start using Herceptin when at the time it had been used exclusively for breast cancer.

A man sitting across the room from me, someone I didn't know, seemed to perk up, and he began asking me some very sensible questions about my treatment and cancer pathology and Her2 amplification. From the detail of his queries, I assumed he was an oncologist.

I asked him if he was. "No," he said, but he added nothing more, as if he were dismissing my question. We moved into the dining room for dinner, and I thought nothing more of it.

When dessert was being served, he walked up to me and introduced himself.

Shahid Imran, it turned out, was a statistician turned molecular biologist, not an oncologist. He was working at Rutgers University after a startup he cofounded in Germany for genetic testing of cancer had folded. He was trying to start a new company doing the same thing in Princeton.

Shahid Imran would turn my entire perception of cancer and cancer treatment on its ear. Sometimes it takes a completely different view of things—a new perspective from a totally different angle—to shake things up and refocus, perhaps redirect, what you thought was the right path.

Shahid was not an oncologist and may or may not have been conversant with the latest medical procedures and initiatives. He was instead a scientist whose sole focus was on cellular behavior—the molecular structure of cancer cells. He studied why they did what they did. He was intrigued by the biology of cancer cells and how they grew, mutated, functioned, and survived and by extension, how one could kill those cells.

As a result, he knew much about the minute details of cancer cell behavior that few oncologists focused on. I was in luck again.

As we sat over our plates of a potpourri of delicious desserts, he asked if he could test my cancer cells, and with that simple question, he set me on a path to learn as much as I could about cutting-edge technologies and immunotherapy—and the fascinating world of mutations that keep repeat-customer cancer cells killing and behaving badly.

Without that chance dinner meeting, it would have taken me much longer to understand that cancer cells have many more mutations than I knew. I had thought before our conversation that there were perhaps eight or nine common ones, when there were hundreds.

If doctors can pinpoint exactly what mutation they are fighting in a specific cancer, the battle becomes more focused and more efficient—which of course is the beauty of targeted treatment. If you know precisely what you are fighting—and today's testing is sophisticated enough to search out and identify hundreds of different mutations—you can attempt to target it specifically.

It starts with this premise, simplified: Cancer takes a normal cell and changes it or mutates it. A normal cell grows, performs its job, and dies in a predetermined pattern, just as we shed skin, for example. A mutation changes all that. The mutated cells will multiply and grow at a rapid rate, refuse to die "a natural death," aggressively attack and destroy the normal tissues, spread all over the body, and eventually kill the patient unless successfully treated.

The mutation process is sophisticated enough to allow cancer to camouflage itself from the body's powerful immune defenses. Those little devils.

If we can find the specific mutation, though, we can try to learn the ways to attack it specifically. The big problem is that we are far behind in the drug research and development area. We can search for and identify hundreds of mutations, if present, in a given cancer. But currently, only a few drugs have been developed to combat a handful of mutations.

Of course, that would change over the next few years.

Medicine has taken great strides to distance itself from what was the Dark Ages for cancer treatment. I was there when I first began my own fight. Today I'm on the cutting edge of a treatment explosion.

In August 2014, as I had feared and expected, my cancer broke through. New lesions appeared and existing ones started growing again. After twenty months—the same length of time it took when the cancer was in my lungs—the Herceptin began losing its effect. The smart, cunning, and insidious cancer had learned to get around it

As I continued to learn more about cell biology—how cancer behaves at that level—I realized how clever and cunning an adversary it was. It was not unlike watching an old horror film. The hero lops off the head of a monster and thinks he's attained victory, but the monster simply grows another head.

The most significant mutation, among many, in my cancer was called PIK3CA. At that time, there were two medicines on the market that targeted this particular mutation.

But those medicines were not approved to treat metastatic salivary duct cancer. The FDA had approved their use only for certain kidney cancers and some breast cancers. I was left out in the cold yet again. Because of that, my health insurance would not pay for it. Without insurance, I'd be forced to pay approximately $6,000 to $8,000 a month—and that was assuming I could find someone to prescribe and administer those drugs to me for a use not authorized by the FDA. It was an impossible situation.

In November 2014, I went back to Memorial Sloan Kettering because I knew that the doctors there in that revered bastion of cancer research would be well acquainted with the latest concepts to view cancer as it was: unique to each patient. Not all breast cancers were the same, not all parotid cancers were the same, and not all lung cancers were the same. A cancer's treatment should be based on its unique features, not on which body area it happened to reside in.

I was hoping to get enrolled in some clinical study testing a new drug to target the PIK3CA mutation. I could then get the medicine free of cost. Unfortunately, that hope was squashed very quickly. In most cancers, the lesions are considered "measurable." The researchers can accurately measure any change in the size of the tumor in millimeters through the entire duration of the study. The doctors could see if it was growing or shrinking. This was not so in my case. Cancers confined to the bones are impossible to measure with such pinpoint accuracy. The lesions in a bone scan may take forever to disappear even after the cancer has regressed. The researchers simply cannot precisely and accurately monitor the response to experimental drugs.

So, I was not a good candidate for a clinical study.

"However, if your cancer spreads to a soft tissue, say liver, then we can enroll you in some study protocol." Hardly a comforting thought.

As I was going over the situation with the doctor at Sloan, he turned to me as he reviewed my records and said, "Did you know that your cancer has receptors for androgens?"

He was referring to the fact that my specific cancer seemed to need male hormones to grow. It was just like some breast cancers require the female hormone, estrogen, to grow.

"Yes," I said. "I do in fact know that."

"Well, has anyone suggested to you that we should try to block the male hormones in your body? That would reduce or maybe even completely deprive the cancer of what it needs to grow."

I smiled.

"Yes. I suggested that eight years ago," I said.

"What happened?" he asked.

"You said no."

"Well, eight years is an eternity in cancer treatment and thinking can change. I think we should try this approach," he said a bit sheepishly.

"I think it might be worthwhile to try," I said.

I returned to Dr. Sharma, and she started me on an aggressive treatment to block the male hormones in my body—and thus deprive my cancer of yet another thing it needed to thrive.

Four months later, scans showed the cancer had stopped growing.

We had hit the spot again.

In May 2015, I suggested to Dr. Sharma that we add another medicine to my treatment regimen. I had seen a recent study that showed breast cancer patients who were Her2 positive—as was I—had reacted even more positively to a combination of Herceptin and another very similar but newer drug, Perjeta. The two drugs used together were more effective than using either alone. There was a synergy between those two drugs.

Dr. Sharma, of course, had read that study too and, as always, was most kind and ever receptive to my suggestions. In October 2015, five months after we introduced Perjeta, my scans revealed that the cancer was not only stable but might actually be showing the slightest sign of regression.

Though it was only a small glimmer of hope, I'd take it.

Today, as I write this in October 2016, that tiny glimmer of hope is burning much brighter. I am completely symptom free now, and the scans continue to indicate a slight but distinct improving trend.

The fight goes on.

BRIGHT HOPE ON THE HORIZON

November 2016

Let's be realistic. There is never a good time to have cancer.

Even today, caution and years of fighting to beat the odds against surviving this insidious enemy have made it an almost certainty that no doctor will ever tell you that the cancer will never return. You may become cancer-free, but no one in the medical establishment will ever say, "You are permanently cured."

And you will learn that protocol as well. I certainly did.

You will learn, in the good times, to say, "I'm cancer-free," or "My cancer is in remission." And you will hope the remission is permanent, but you will keep that to yourself.

You will not dare say, "I'm cured. It's gone. I beat it. It will never return."

It could be back next week or next year or in five years or never. Yes, in an increasing number of cancer patients, the fight does get won and cancer never returns. But it takes fifteen or twenty years of being cancer free before you can even begin to entertain that thought. You just never know, and you never forget that harsh fact. Those are the unstated rules for being a certified member of the Cancer Club, and you learn them very quickly.

Fine.

I learned those rules as a physician and got personally reacquainted during my own struggle, so in due course, I learned to play by them. But the more years I survived and the more knowledge I gained, the more I got calls from friends and friends of friends of friends.

"How did you do it?" they asked. "What should I do?"

Very few people have been lucky enough to escape being touched in some way by cancer. They have a friend or a brother or a mother who died, they have an uncle who is in serious condition, or they know the nice woman down the street who was just diagnosed.

I'm happy to be where I am today—a survivor for many years. I'm gratified that people come to me for answers about what to do.

Now, today, this is what I can tell them.

We are tantalizingly close to being able to say we have cured a particular cancer.

What makes this hope shine even brighter is that this is happening in a few different areas, so beating cancer does not hinge on just one idea or just one drug or one group of scientists. There are several prongs in this latest assault on cancer, coming from teams of researchers and doctors working on different theories in different parts of the world with astonishing results. This can mean only good news, because it means the assault is coming from all sides.

It is as if cancer is now surrounded by elite troops and has little chance to escape.

Medical science has made extraordinary strides in understanding this horrible disease that has killed so many people while the doctors often seemed powerless to do anything about it.

Today, finally, researchers are beginning to understand the nuances of how cancer does what it does, so they can focus on developing methods to beat it.

Recent progress in medical research has dwarfed that of even the last few years—when the medical community was astonished at how much it was learning and how fast it was moving forward in the battle.

Some of the things happening in the battle against cancer today sound like pure science fiction—unbelievable hoopla.

Today, we can look back on how we treated cancer as recently as the 1990s and equate it with the Dark Ages—a time when very little was really understood. By comparison to what we know today, treatments thought to be cutting edge in the 1970s and 1980s seem downright primitive.

In the 1960s and 1970s, for example, doctors treated cancer in a one-size-fits-all manner. There were only a handful of cytotoxic chemotherapy drugs used to treat every form of cancer—and usually they had horrible, debilitating side effects. More often than not, a cancer diagnosis was a death sentence.

In the 1980s, things began to change a bit. Doctors would treat breast cancer differently than say, lung cancer, which would be treated differently than kidney or bone cancer.

But that was missing the point as well.

Over time, doctors began to realize that it didn't matter where the cancer began. They saw that each cancer had its own particular histology and its own unique behavior.

My cancer is a classic example. It started in the parotid gland but, under the microscope, looked just like the ductal carcinoma of the breast. The fact that it originated from the parotid gland, not the breast, is rather irrelevant. It is basically the same cancer and should be treated the same way. And later, when it spread to the lungs or the bones, it was still the same parotid cancer, not a lung cancer or a bone cancer. It just happened to relocate there.

My cancer had a life of its own. It was unique. It did not matter where it started from or where it migrated to.

Once doctors began to see that, researchers were at the dawn of the new concept of targeted therapies. Each cancer was unique to each patient. The treatment should be individualized, targeted, against that particular cancer based on its unique characteristics, behavior, and vulnerabilities. One size does not fit all.

I would like to think—hope in fact—that no future cancer patients will have to fight the way I did to get certain treatments, that doctors today could help them prevent that. This novel concept, originated by some diligent medical researchers and innovators, is now universally accepted by oncologists.

The problem is that federal agencies and the health insurers are still stuck in the past. My cancer, the salivary duct carcinoma of the parotid is practically a twin of the ductal carcinoma of the breast. It stands to reason that a drug that worked against one is likely to work against the other too. Because breast cancer is very common and parotid cancer is exceedingly rare, it is far, far easier for researchers and drug companies to test a new drug against breast cancer than against parotid cancer. Therefore, they can present convincing data to the FDA to show that a particular new drug works against breast cancer and thus get the approval for its use in breast cancer treatment. Unfortunately, parotid cancer patients, due to their small numbers, are left out in the cold. There are plenty of drugs that are FDA approved for use for breast cancer but none for parotid cancer. This allows the health insurers to refuse payment for most new drugs for patients like me. It becomes an uphill battle, often futile, to fight. I am blessed to have had the wherewithal I did, but not everyone survives the fight.

The simple logic is that if a drug blocks Her2 and successfully treats Her2-positive breast cancer, its use should be approved for any cancer anywhere that is Her2 positive. Unfortunately, this simple logic is lost on many in the hierarchy. This, I hope, will change in due time.

We should not be hung up on where that cancer was found. We should be looking at it under the microscope and analyzing it in the laboratory to see how it behaves and then customizing a treatment program. And that is what is happening today. With radical and powerful developments now being used, it will send the old methods into the distant past, never to be thought of again.

We are almost there today. The medical community, oncologists, and researchers know that. It is high time for the regulators and insurers to get with the program.

I think of the whole thing in this way: The evolution of cancer treatment is similar to the evolution of how we used telephones. Years ago, in the 1940s and 1950s, we had neighbors sharing the same line, first the crank-up type and then old rotary phones—party lines they were called. It would not be unusual to pick up the phone and learn that your next-door neighbor was already talking on it. You would have to wait—and hope that your neighbor would not blather on for another hour before you could make your call.

Later, we began to see home phones—one house, one line. But still, everyone in the house was on the same line. If you picked it up to make a call, you might hear your brother talking to his girlfriend. You couldn't get on until he hung up.

Today we have cell phones and the days of the house phone are almost over; the concept of a party line is simply laughable.

Cells phones of today are highly personalized and sophisticated communication tools. They are configured exactly to specific users' specifications: their own phone number; the exact amount of memory they need; the number and kinds of apps they want installed; their contact list; their choice of songs, photos, videos, and documents; and even their very personal and confidential data. It is a highly personalized gadget now.

So is cancer treatment.

And that wonderful news is why if there were a better time to have cancer, to have a doctor drop the bad news on you, it is today—right now.

Why is this happening?

On one front, medical science continues to make extraordinary strides. Each new kernel of knowledge accelerates and expands what was previously known—one new discovery leads to five more. Targeted therapy is one example—but a very good one.

On a second front, doctors have begun to expand their knowledge about how to marshal the body's own defenses, its own immune system, to attack cancer.

Former President Jimmy Carter astounded the world in December 2015 when he announced he was cancer free. Only months before, he had said it was unlikely he would survive the late-stage malignant melanoma that had spread to his brain.

He might have astonished the general public, but medical insiders were not as surprised. Mr. Carter was the beneficiary of a new wonder drug, Nivolumab, and the relatively new concept of immunotherapy for cancer—checkpoint blockade.

We all are familiar with the miracle of modern antibiotics. Most infections, even the serious and life-threatening kind, can usually be cured by the proper use of antibiotics. But antibiotics cannot work without help from the patient's immune system.

Every day, literally hundreds of times a day, various bacteria and viruses invade our bodies. Yet, we are not constantly sick. Why? Because our immune system is always on guard, ready to fight and destroy every potential enemy. The invaders are promptly killed and the threat is eliminated without us ever becoming aware of it.

It is only when the bacteria manage to establish a beachhead that we show signs of illness. Even then, the immune system plays a critical role in helping the antibiotics conquer the infection. Antibiotics simply cannot work if the immune system is diseased and unable to help, as in HIV. That is precisely why in HIV even a minor infection can threaten the patient's life despite the use of antibiotics. Our immune system is the most powerful, sophisticated, efficient, and elite fighting army one can imagine.

So, why does it not fight the cancer and kill it off? For decades, medical scientists have struggled with precisely this question. Why was the immune system actually ignoring the horrid invasion? Why was it sitting quietly by while the cancer invaded and destroyed one vital organ after another until it killed the patient?

It has been only in the last few years that we have realized what was happening.

Cancer is wily and cunning. That, of course, is not a surprise. But researchers have begun to understand that cancer cells actually make themselves invisible to the immune system. We still do not have a complete understanding as to how, but we have learned a few things.

This we do know: The immune system fights off various invasions through a system of checkpoints. Say, for example, you have strep throat. When the germs first invade, an alarm is triggered which serves to mobilize the body's immune forces. They attack the strep germs and kill them off. Soon, the immune forces reach a checkpoint where they must stop to receive fresh orders. If the threat persists, the order will be to continue the attack. On the other hand, if the threat has been eliminated, that information will be conveyed to the immune forces, thereby shutting them down. Obviously, we do not want our army to keep firing after the enemy is dead. It will only cause harm to the civilians. Similarly, our immune system must not go on unchecked in order to prevent damage to the normal and healthy tissues.

So, our immune response is a pattern of repeated starts and stops regulated by a series of checkpoints.

Scientists have learned that cancer has the ability to trigger checkpoints or manipulate the checkpoint signals. As soon as the immune forces attack the cancer, it initiates a checkpoint signal to terminate that immune response. Cancer has a way of making the checkpoint say—to continue the analogy—"No problems here. The threat is gone. All clear now."

So far, we only know about a couple of different ways this is accomplished. But it is very likely that the wily cancer has many other ways to fool the immune system. Our knowledge is still growing by the day.

Once scientists understood that mechanism, they began to develop medicines that neutralized the false checkpoint signals created by the cancer, thus allowing the immune system to continue to attack and kill the cancer cells. These drugs are called checkpoint blockade therapies.

In clinical trials, these medicines have produced a 66 percent success rate against an extremely deadly cancer, malignant melanoma. This is an astonishing success, and we may even improve upon that success as we learn to use different drug combinations and newer and better drugs are developed. Each day brings the dawn of a new hope.

Another prong in the battle that has brought jaw-dropping positive results is something called adoptive T-cell transfer. This is the stuff of science fiction. And the exciting results it is producing have turned cancer research on its ears.

Using T-cells to kill cancer will put medicine on the cusp of being able to say we have found a cure for cancer. Adoptive T-cell transfer therapy is the most promising technique we have to finally attain the Holy Grail of cancer medicine—to be able to utter those three magical words to the patient: "You are cured!"

T-cells are our immune system's killer cells. Think of them in a way as an elite commando force that can seek out and destroy the enemy. The challenge is this: because of mechanisms we are still trying to fully understand, cancer cells camouflage themselves from T-cells. So, how do you make the T-cells "see" this enemy called cancer? If they can see it, they will attack it and destroy it.

In February 2014, two groups of scientists in New York City presented the early data of what can only be described as a phenomenal study with phenomenal results.

In a study using sixteen adult leukemia patients, scientists took samples of each patient's T-cells and samples of his or her cancer cells. Under laboratory conditions, they trained those T-cells to recognize certain specific traits of that patient's leukemia cell and then attack to kill it—it was like teaching a drug-sniffing dog to find the cache of hero-in. These were called "smart T-cells."

The next step was crucial, dangerous, and amazingly clever.

The researchers cloned millions of these specially trained T-cells and then went back to the patients and gave them very toxic chemicals that destroyed their "dumb" T-cells—those that were still fooled by the cancer's camou-flaging. They then replaced them with the trained smart T-cells.

It was certainly a very, very dangerous procedure—but it was necessary.

Once infused, the trained T-cells set out like an elite commando force equipped with exact GPS coordinates and hunted down and killed the cancer cells.

The success rate of achieving a complete response was an astounding 88 percent!

The incredible success of that small study, and a few others since, has sparked an explosion of interest and further studies by various medical centers and pharma-ceutical companies worldwide, who are spending billions of dollars in similar research. These investments are sure to be returned many times over, of course. But it can only mean good things for cancer patients. Costs for adop-tive T-cell transfer treatments now are prohibitive for in-dividuals—as much as $500,000 for one patient, which is totally unacceptable. But that will change in the near future.

And there were complications, of course, with ominous results for one patient.

In one unfortunate patient, a man from New York City with Her2-positive colorectal cancer, doctors infused T-cells trained to seek out and kill Her2-positive cancer cells. The man went into respiratory arrest within fifteen minutes. His health continued to deteriorate over the next few days despite the best efforts of the medical experts. He died after four days when his lungs shut down completely. There was nothing they could do to save the patient.

An autopsy showed that the patient's normal lung cells had traces of Her2. The "smart" T-cells had been attacking and killing the healthy lung tissues as well as the cancer.

These trained T-cells are like heat-seeking missiles. They will attack and kill as they have been trained to do—and there was no reversing this once they were set loose.

You lose any control over the missile once it is fired.

This unfortunate incident led to a temporary halt of all further experimentation in this area. The focus was shifted to try to find a way to control these smart T-cells after they were infused into the patient's bloodstream. How do you stop these commandos if they go rogue? How do you destroy a wayward missile?

A few different strategies are being developed to accomplish that. One of those is the development of what is called a "suicide gene"—and it is truly the stuff of science fiction. Now scientists can tag T-cells with this suicide gene. If they go haywire and start attacking normal cells, doctors can prompt them to destroy themselves, or commit suicide.

It is nothing short of amazing. Today we are on the cusp of advances that were not even imagined just a few years ago. No, when someone disconsolately calls me for advice and tells me they have been given no more than two years to live, I tell them not to panic or lose hope. I emphasized that two years is an eternity when it comes to medical advances, the way science is exploding in its efforts to cure cancer.

"Take heart," I tell them. "Every year, new drugs and modalities are being developed. In two or three years, you have no idea what new miracle drug may come out." I suggest optimism and advise they focus on positive thoughts, avoid negativity and depression, refuse to panic, eat healthily, remain physically active, meditate, enjoy every little pleasure in life, and, as much as possible, avoid stress. Most of all, do not give up hope.

All that will boost your immune system and will go a long way toward beating this dangerous enemy.

Two years—or even a year—given the ways that science is moving ahead, is a terrific pronouncement. This, in no way, is meant to paint an unrealistically rosy picture. Cancer has been and continues to be an extremely deadly disease. Even though the death rate from cancer has gradually and steadily declined since 1990, there are still far too many patients dying from it. In the United States, cancer continues to be the second biggest cause of death, behind heart disease only. Over half a million patients die from cancer each year in the United States alone. More than eight million lives are lost worldwide.

I am fully aware of all that. Yet, there is no doubt that we are entering a much better and far more hopeful era. At no other time in the history of medicine have we been this tantalizingly close to achieving a major victory against cancer, a game-changing victory that will forever change the cancer outlook.

I believe this with all my heart.

In a few short years, in the very near future, we might be hearing a doctor finally say those magic words: "You are cured of cancer."

YOU HAVE CANCER—
NOW WHAT?

Take a deep, calming breath. Exhale slowly.

Your worst fears are confirmed. You had been hoping that your discomfort and troubling symptoms were something that would pass, that you'd wake up one morning and they would have suddenly disappeared—and everything would be back to normal.

But the test results are back. Your doctor has confirmed you have cancer. For a while anyway, nothing will be normal.

What next?

Your biggest ally in this upcoming fight is your attitude—your emotional reaction. Adopt eternal optimism and install an unshakeable belief that you can and will fight this enemy. Put on your armor and fight. Medical studies show that positive thinking triggers your immune system into action while negative thoughts and despair shut it down. Successful treatment of cancer requires a joint effort. Your doctors will do their job, but you, the patient, must do yours. Without your help, it is an uphill battle.

As you settle into what could be a lengthy period of treatment, you must first relax. A cancer diagnosis is not the end of the world. Recognize you are not alone and know there is a world of support waiting for you. You are about to be challenged in a number of ways on a number of fronts.

Here are some suggestions about how to proceed in a way that will allow you to take advantage of the many resources available and address the various assaults that will come from what seems every direction. There are four basic areas you will need to recognize: physical, emotional, practical, and financial.

Physical and Emotional
Your doctor will begin by recommending a treatment.

- Get a second or third opinion. Get a fourth if you're still not satisfied.

Remember that this is your life they are speaking about, and now is not the time to concern yourself with hurt feelings. A good physician, a confident physician, will not be offended if you say you want other opinions on how to proceed. Keep asking questions until you are satisfied you have a handle on a treatment plan you are comfortable with. Even if you like your oncologist, another oncologist might recommend a different path. If a doctor is offended by your desire to seek a second opinion, he or she is not the right one.

Have thorough discussions with your physicians, multiple times if you are not satisfied. If a doctor doesn't have time to listen and communicate to your satisfaction, find another one immediately. Discover and discuss all possible options for treatment.

- Seek the ivory towers.

These institutions are so named because they attract the best and the brightest. They are on the cutting edge of new treatments and new ideas. Places like Memorial Sloan Kettering, Dana-Farber, the Mayo Clinic, Johns Hopkins, and literally dozens of other centers are often looking for patients to participate in studies. Pick up the phone and call. You might be surprised how easy it is to speak to someone.

- Be vigilant and proactive.

Do not waste time, and don't let your doctors waste time. They are only human, and they do make mistakes. Being vigilant does not mean being a hypochondriac or a nervous Nelly. Vigilance is especially important, critical actually, after what appears to be a successful round of treatment.

- Do not panic.

Cancer is not the automatic death sentence it once was. In a vast majority of cases, it can be treated. Even if it comes back—metastatic cancer—it can often be converted to a situation that is perhaps not curable but manageable.

- Have faith.

Do not get too hung up on the diagnosed cancer stage, even if it is advanced. Patients with stage III and IV have successful outcomes all the time. I am living proof.

- Do your own research.

Go online and read as much as you can. Talk to the extended community of other patients just like you. Use social media. Go to WebMD, national cancer institutes, Wikipedia, or professional organizations. Be aware, though, of Dr. Google! Ignore nonprofessionals or those who have something to sell.

- Follow instructions.

Be religious and faithful about what you are told to do. Do not change anything or add anything, like "natural remedies" before talking to your doctor. Do not modify your prescriptions without consulting your doctor.

A Word about Alternative Therapies
Most doctors are very open to these as long as there is no known conflict with your prescribed drugs. Try to find those with some scientific data to support their claimed efficacy. Remember, "natural" does not always mean "harmless" (poisonous mushrooms, for example). Do not give up

scientifically proven treatment to chase after nonscientific ones. Do not waste time.

- Stay positive. Do not give up.

Always stay positive. Never give up hope. Never stop fighting. Never get too down and depressed even if the prognosis for survival seems only a couple of years. A lot can happen. Medical science is advancing at breakneck speed in cancer research. Childhood leukemia, once universally fatal, is now always treatable and possibly curable. Glioblastoma multiforme, a most deadly brain tumor, with an average survival of only fifteen months just a couple of years ago, has a more hopeful prognosis now, with some patients surviving for years. And even better treatments are on the horizon.

Getting depressed or anxious or panic-stricken is a natural reaction. Get all the emotional support you can get. Lean on family and friends. Talk to your doctors and nurses about your emotional health. Seek out psychological help if you are overwhelmed. Antianxiety and antidepressant medicines for short-term use can be immensely valuable, and they can help you maintain the emotional strength you need to survive. I have found that escitalopram (Lexapro) is uniquely beneficial when started early in the course of chemo or radiation therapy. It alleviates anxiety, elevates the mood, and reduces chronic pain. It worked for me.

- Pour your heart out. Talk to anyone who will listen. Remember, if I had not shown up at that wedding and run into my old friend from medical school, my journey may have taken a very different path.

Now is not the time to be heroically stoic. There is no weakness in leaning on others around you. Let your loved ones know how you feel, that you might be frightened about what is going on. Get as much support, emotional and physical, as you can. There is strength in numbers. Know that the friends and loved ones who are surrounding you and helping you will do immeasurably positive things for you.

Practical

- Ask for help.

Get rides to chemo treatments or doctors' appointments. Have friends and family buy groceries, move furniture, or run errands. You will be surprised how many people are waiting for you to ask. They want to help in any way they can. Let them.

- Let people at work know.

Talk to your boss. Let him or her know what is going on. Ask for a lighter load or concessions on your schedule or to work from home on certain days. If necessary, ask for extended time off while you go through treatment.

Financial

- Make it personal.

Treatment is not cheap. If you can, establish a personal relationship with your insurance company, and do so early in the process. Find out what they will cover and how much; fight for exceptions, such as new studies. Try to avoid last-minute surprises about what is covered and what is not. Communicate with your doctors and their staff and enlist their help in dealing with insurers. Don't automatically accept a ruling on what is covered and what is not.

- Talk to family.

Don't be shy or too proud to ask family members who can to help with money.

- Look for funding.

There are nonprofit foundations that might have the resources and means to help you. Seek them out. If, for one example, the FDA approves a drug for your type of cancer but insurance will pay poorly or none at all, you might be able to find a nonprofit that will pay for it. Even the drug manufacturers have various plans to help you defray the cost of these extremely expensive drugs Many manufacturers can provide you with coupons and discounts they do not publicly advertise. You may want to explore the Internet fundraising resources such as GoFundMe.

Be well. Stay healthy. Keep learning. Never give up. Stay positive, and may peace always be with you!

Made in the USA
Middletown, DE
08 March 2017